MEDITATION IS A safe, secure way for you to explore both the inner workings of your own mind and the outer manifestations of transcendental reality. Along the way you will meet your own personality and make friends with all its facets—good, bad, or otherwise. You will also touch the larger nature of the Universe in ways that are profoundly comforting and healing. You will develop patience with yourself and others. Finally, you will gain insights from your contemplative experience that cannot be obtained any other way.

— Stephanie Clement

About the Author

Stephanie Clement has an M.A. in humanistic psychology and a Ph.D. in transpersonal psychology. She is a professional astrologer and is a member of the board of directors of the American Federation of Astrologers. Stephanie is also a certified hypnotherapist and a faculty member of Kepler College.

To Write to the Author

If you wish to contact the author or would like more information about this book, please write to the author in care of Llewellyn Worldwide and we will forward your request. Both the author and publisher appreciate hearing from you and learning of your enjoyment of this book and how it has helped you. Llewellyn Worldwide cannot guarantee that every letter written to the author can be answered, but all will be forwarded. Please write to:

Stephanie Clement, Ph.D.
% Llewellyn Worldwide
2143 Wooddale Drive, Dept. 978-0-7387-0203-2
Woodbury, MN 55125-2989, U.S.A.

Please enclose a self-addressed stamped envelope for reply,
or $1.00 to cover costs. If outside U.S.A., enclose
international postal reply coupon.

Many of Llewellyn's authors have websites with additional information and resources. For more information, please visit our website at:

http://www.llewellyn.com

Meditation
for Beginners

Techniques for Awareness,
Mindfulness & Relaxation

Stephanie Clement, Ph.D.

Llewellyn Publications
Woodbury, Minnesota

First Edition
Tenth Printing, 2010

Book design and editing by Joanna Willis
Cover photograph © 2007 by Colin Anderson/Blend Images/PunchStock
Cover design by Adrienne Zimiga
Illustrations on pages 25–27, 29, 95, and 117 by Gavin Dayton Duffy,
   Llewellyn art department
Illustration on page 116 by Kevin R. Brown, Llewellyn art department

Library of Congress Cataloging-in-Publication Data
Clement, Stephanie Jean.
   Meditation for beginners: techniques for awareness, mindfulness &
   relaxation / Stephanie Clement.— 1st ed.
        p.   cm.
   Includes bibliographical references and index.
   ISBN 13: 978-0-7387-0203-2
   ISBN 10: 0-7387-0203-X
   1. Meditation. I. Title.

BL627 .C58 2002
158.1'2—dc21

2002070229

Llewellyn Publications
A Division of Llewellyn Worldwide, Ltd.
2143 Woodale Drive, Dept. 978-0-7387-0203-2
Woodbury, MN 55125-2989, U.S.A.
www.llewellyn.com
Llewellyn is a registered trademark of Llewellyn Worldwide, Ltd.
Printed in the United States of America

*This book is dedicated to the long lives of
His Holiness the XIV Dalai Lama and
His Holiness the XVII Karmapa.
May their beneficial influence fill the world
with peace, wisdom, and joy.*

Also by Stephanie Clement

Charting Your Career

Charting Your Spiritual Path with Astrology

Civilization Under Attack
(editor)

Dreams: Working Interactive

Power of the Midheaven

What Astrology Can Do for You

Contents

Contents

Contents

Contents

Exercises

What Exactly Is Meditation Anyway?

*[In meditation] consciousness shifts increasingly into aware-
ness of that which is not form and into the realm of that
which is transcendent or into the world of the abstract, i.e.,
into that which is abstracted from form and focused in itself.*

Alice Bailey
Esoteric Astrology

IT IS EASIER to say what meditation is not. Meditation is not relaxing in your recliner to watch Sunday
football games. Meditation is not becoming hypnotized by
the dotted lines on the pavement while driving. Meditation is not sitting and staring out the window instead of
doing your work.

The process of meditation as discussed in this book is
about focusing attention, not thoughts. In some systems, it
is not even about focusing attention, but about relaxing

1

the mind and body instead. Because there are many ways to meditate and many potential goals for meditation, there is no one definition that suits all the possibilities.

Definitions from the dictionary tell us about the properties associated with meditation. The first definition in the tenth edition of *Webster's Collegiate Dictionary* is not about meditating at all, but has to do with the result of meditation or reflecting. It states that "meditation is a discourse intended to express its author's reflections or to guide others in contemplation." It is a work written after one has considered the subject deeply, and for the use of others.

The second definition is not much more helpful. It tells us that meditation is the "act or process of meditating." Hmm, we already knew that. So what does "meditate" mean?

"Meditate" comes from the Latin word *meditari,* and means "to engage in contemplation or reflection." It also means "to focus one's thoughts" on something, or "to reflect on or ponder" over something. A third definition is "to plan or project in the mind," to intend, or to develop one's purpose. So far the most helpful is the bit about focusing one's thoughts, but that is not the true intention of meditation either. The definition for the word "meditate" in the ninth edition of *Webster's New College Dictionary* mentions the Latin word *mete,* which means "boundary." The tenth edition of *Webster's Collegiate Dictionary* mentions the Latin word *mederi,* which means "to remedy, heal" (it is the root of the word *medical*), and the Greek word *medesthai,* which means "to be mindful of."

At first blush, these definitions don't do much to help explain how to meditate. In fact, the definitions are very misleading. Let's take a look, though, at the words *intend* and *purpose* from above. For most of us, everything we do has some intention. We don't spend much time acting without purpose. If I am to convince you that meditation is a good thing, I need to be very clear about its purpose. I need to convince you that you can achieve some worthwhile goals through meditation.

Now let's consider the phrase "to be mindful of," or simply "to be mindful." This is more like it. Meditation is sometimes called mindfulness training or training the mind. Instead of letting it go wherever it chooses, we can train our minds to focus.

Meditation is about relaxing the mind, focusing attention, and fulfilling a purpose or goal. This book explores these three areas:

1. You will find a variety of ways to relax the body and mind.

2. You will learn about focusing your attention, and you can practice the exercises found throughout the book.

3. You will find suggested purposes for meditation, along with goals that you may achieve as you meditate.

So what's this business about boundaries? How does that fit into the meditation picture? When we think about ourselves, we tend to think that each of us is separate. "I live inside my body/mind, and the rest of the world is outside. I prescribe a boundary around myself." Such a boundary is not entirely logical. Each time I breathe, I inhale air that has, for the most part, been through someone else's lungs. I eat food that has been cycled and recycled. In my daily interactions with others, I seek to make connections so that I feel less separate. Yet I have this self-made boundary between myself and others.

We set boundaries for everything. My house is a boundary between me and the cold. My yard has a boundary that was legally set when the land around me was subdivided. Nations have boundaries. Corporations have boundaries described in law by patent, copyright, and so on. We are all about boundaries. Or are we?

In his poem "Mending Wall," Robert Frost writes, "Something there is that doesn't love a wall." Later in the same poem he suggests, "Before I built a wall I'd ask to know/What I was walling in or walling out,/And to whom I was like to give offense." Frost is asking, "Why do I need this boundary of a wall between me and my neighbor?" You could ask yourself the same question about any "wall" between you and others, or between your own conscious and unconscious experience.

One goal of meditation is to understand the boundaries we have set for ourselves. Perhaps the greatest boundary— and certainly the toughest—is the one we set between the conscious and less conscious parts of our own minds. No single activity requires as much of us as the assault on that barrier. Each day we go about our conscious waking life, and each night the unconscious speaks to us in the form of dreams, enticing us to deeper self-understanding. Then each day we rebuild the boundary. We all need a way to gain a deeper understanding of what goes on inside our minds when we are awake, asleep, or just not paying attention, and meditation is one way to pay attention long enough to find out.

Let's explore how boundaries work through some of the systems in our lives. We tend to think of our lives as consisting of separate units that interact with each other, yet remain independent. An example is the family. I grew up in a household that included my parents and siblings. Eventually my grandmother came to live with us. Before she lived in our house, she was like a separate unit. Once she lived in our house, she came to be defined as a member of our nuclear family. She took an active role in household management, and she read to us, talked with us, and scolded us just like our parents. She went to concerts with us, shared the crossword puzzles in the newspaper with my father, and took vacations with my mother. When she later moved out of our house, she ceased to be part of the nuclear group and returned to her former status of "close relative."

Does the distinction feel artificial? How could we just move Grandma in and out of the nuclear family system? The door of our house was the defining boundary. All persons who lived on the other side of our door were not part of the nuclear family.

---

exercise

perceiving boundaries

Take a few moments to think of an area of your life that is important to you.

1. Think about the boundaries that you encounter as you think about it.

2. What people, pets, or other things fit within that area of your life?

3. Now think about what happens to those people or things when you are not doing something with them? Do they go across a boundary to become part of another system? Do you cross a boundary yourself?

4. Is the picture becoming complicated? How do you know exactly where the boundary is? Does it move or change depending on circumstances?

Meditation can help you understand the boundaries you have created around yourself. You will come to understand how some boundaries are helpful, and some serve no apparent purpose. In the process you can expect your relationships with other people to change. You can also expect a dramatic change in your understanding of yourself.

Much of the stress you experience in your life is about boundaries. As you understand how systems—conscious, less conscious, social, and economic—interact in your life, you will relax in both body and mind. Meditation provides a way to explore your beliefs about boundaries among different systems.

Your Mental Meditation Equipment

Meditation begins with our perceptions and judgments of the world. We perceive the world through five senses:

sight, sound, taste, smell, and tactile feeling. The limitations of these physical senses necessarily limit our ability to gather information about the world. Using the mind, we judge the world based on what we perceive; we think about the facts and make decisions.

Integration depends on things we cannot perceive with the ordinary senses. We live within the unified system we call the body, and this system is connected to other systems. (For example, you are one member of your family system.) We depend on, are affected by, and respond to many factors within the body that we can't experience through the ordinary senses. (Pulse rate, for example, is something we can readily experience, but generally, blood pressure is not.) How can we relate to these factors? We have three methods of gathering information beyond the senses.

1. We use tools and machines to take measurements for us. We don't need meditation for this one, although meditation in some form was probably involved in the creation of the tool or machine.

2. We use our minds to gather information through thought. Once we have gathered the sensory data, we engage in a thought process designed to make sense of the data—to put it in order or organize it in a useful way. Much of our day-to-day problem solving involves this mental process of examination and sorting. Critical evaluation can then occur.

3. We also gather information through contemplative practice, or the resting of the mind. The process of

meditation often focuses the mind on one thing—*mantra* (words) or *yantra* (visual image) or the breath—to the exclusion of other thoughts. A sort of ritual process is used to get the mind to go in a specified direction. Some meditative practices deliberately clear the mind of thoughts as completely as possible.

While we are all familiar with basic ways to let machines gather information and register it in useful ways, we often forget that we can simply relax and allow our minds to scan remembered information and reorganize it. Even less are we able to use our minds to gather information from outside the stores of "normal" memory.

We think of scientists as using method number one from above, and philosophers as tending toward method number two. The third method is often ignored. Yet Ken Wilber, a leading writer in the transpersonal psychology field, makes a case that all three methods are valid in their own ways.

> Each of the three modes of knowing, then, has access to real (experiential) data in their respective realms—to sensible data, intelligible data, and transcendental data—and the data in each case is marked by its immediate or intuitive apprehension.[1]

We all learn the first way to relate to the world; we use our senses or we gather sensory data from machines. Most of us also learn some theory and philosophy of subjects

---

1. Wilber, *Eye to Eye*, 44.

that interest us, so we are familiar with the second method as well. However, relatively few of us are taught how to gather and evaluate transcendental data. Western religions tend to "can" such information and spoon-feed it to us as though it were scientifically proven fact, when it is no such thing. In *Mission of the University*, Spanish author and philosopher Jose Ortega y Gasset states, "There is no cogent reason why the ordinary man needs or ought to be a scientist."[2] He suggests that we should learn about the physical scheme of our work, themes of organic life, processes of the human species, and finally the plan of the Universe. Note that he presumes there is such a plan. Many religions tell us that the plan can be understood through contemplative practice, but you do not need to engage in organized religion in order to gather information about the world.

Ken Wilber addresses the question of purpose in our lives in the following way:

> The basic Nature of human beings . . . is ultimate Wholeness. This is eternally and timelessly so—that is, true from the beginning, true to the end, and most importantly, true right now, moment to moment to moment. This ever-present and ultimate Wholeness, as it appears in men and women, we call Atman (after the Hindus), or Buddha Nature (after the Buddhists), or Tao, or Spirit, or Consciousness (super-consciousness), or . . . God.[3]

---

2. Ortega y Gasset, *Mission of the University*, 59.
3. Wilber, *Up from Eden*, 12.

Is your perceived meditation goal ultimate wholeness? Maybe not. Still, the transcendent experience is very likely going to occur while you meditate, and your concepts of boundaries will be challenged. It is helpful to understand from the outset that you will not lose your capacity to function within boundaries. Many boundaries are comfortable and they serve definite purposes in our lives. We would be lost without them. What meditation will do is reveal broader experiences of consciousness. You will develop greater flexibility in deciding how to stop reacting and begin responding to the pressures in your life.

Another benefit of meditation is an alteration of self-image. We define our position in the world through the boundary between self and other. The paradox is that while you may feel very separate and different from others, this is a false distinction. We are not separate from each other, even though you are reading this page and I am (physically) far away. We are actually significant "parts" or members of the same unified, complete, and perfect whole. In fact, we are co-determinant with the Universe. We are not so much separate parts of the Universe as we are distinct facets of one larger system.

exercise
_____

perceiving systems

1. Remember the blocks kids play with? Sometimes they come in bright colors, and sometimes they just have different shapes. Some are larger than others. Yet they are all part of the set of blocks.

2. Think about the pieces on a chessboard. They serve individual functions, yet they are all chess pieces.

3. Think of individual people within the larger set of humanity, which is within the larger set of vertebrates, which is within the still larger set of living things.

Even as we recognize this "wheels-within-wheels" view of the world, we need a self-concept in order to survive in the physical world. I need to distinguish between what is mainly inside my mind and what is outside it, and so do you. The paradox of ultimate wholeness and individuality is that both are fundamentally true and real and desirable. We may want to stick to the scientific method of understanding, but we are continually surprised by the world and its workings. We examine the trees, and are startled to find ourselves deep in the forest.

<hr>

summary

Meditation is a safe, secure way for you to explore both the inner workings of your own mind and the outer manifestations of transcendental reality. Along the way you will meet your own personality and make friends with all its facets—good, bad, or otherwise. You will also touch the larger nature of the Universe in ways that are profoundly comforting and healing. You will develop patience with yourself and others. Finally, you will gain insights from your contemplative experience that cannot be obtained any other way.

Going back to the image of the wall, it is my hope that through meditation, you are able to discern the walls you have constructed within your own mind and between yourself and the world. Also, through meditation I hope you begin to discover the doorways through these obstacles.

Why Meditate?

No one has ever plumbed the depths of either the conscious or the subjective life. In both directions we reach out to Infinity.

Ernest Holmes
The Science of Mind

IF YOU ARE reading this first chapter of this book, you have probably already asked the question, "Why meditate?" You might also have some ideas about why you want to explore meditation further. Maybe your friends have tried it and you've seen some beneficial changes in them. Perhaps your doctor has suggested that you find ways to relieve stress. You may have heard something about it in a class or workshop and decided to get more information. This chapter lists different reasons why people begin meditating, as well as the short- and long-term results you can expect from it.

The most basic result of meditation is an altered state of consciousness. Actually, this result is not difficult to achieve, as your state of mind changes from moment to moment anyway. With meditation, however, there is a certain direction that the alteration is expected to take: muscles relax, emotional states become more calm, the mind rests, blood pressure decreases, pulse rate declines, the eyes focus in a different way, breathing slows, and an awareness of sounds in the immediate environment may increase.

If you meditate for an extended period of time, you may become aware of the shifting angle of the sun coming in a window. Your awareness may extend to other people in the room, or to sounds outside the building. Some people have said they can tune in to the movement of the planet itself by lying still on the ground and looking up at the night sky.

If your only meditation goal is relaxation, you will meet a challenge. Yes, your muscles relax, your emotions become quiet, and your heart rate slows. You can achieve measurable stress reduction in this way. On the other hand, the chatter in your mind becomes more and more apparent as you become quiet. Also, after an extended period of sitting in a meditative posture, your muscles begin to rebel. You develop twitches, muscles begin to cramp if the posture is unusual, and you fidget. What is meant to be relaxing becomes uncomfortable—sometimes quite uncomfortable.

During extended meditation it is helpful to vary your technique. A period of sitting can be followed by a few minutes of walking to loosen up your muscles. You may think that ten minutes is a long time to sit still, and one minute of walking around is enough to flex and stretch. Often, people sit for forty-five to fifty minutes and walk for ten.

Meditation is not about how much time you put into it. Unless you live in a monastery or ashram, you probably don't have many hours each day to devote to meditation. However, you do have shorter periods of time available. The following are some examples:

- After you come home from school or work and have prepared supper, use the fifteen to twenty minutes while your food is baking in the oven.

- When you are on a plane or train or bus.

- When you are getting a haircut.

- When you are waiting for an appointment.

- When you are in the dentist's chair and waiting for the shot to take effect. (I know, this one will be a challenge for almost everybody!)

- When you are walking, running, or jogging.

- When you are painting, raking leaves, or doing other repetitive work.

By the same token, there are other times when your conscious attention needs to be given to what you are doing, and safety is an issue. Examples include:

- Driving a car

- Weightlifting

- Boiling or frying food

- Using any sharp implements

- Caring for children

- Crossing streets or roads

- Handling breakable objects

- Attending a lecture or performance

- Walking up or down stairs

- Moving furniture

These lists are not exhaustive, but they show that you can find meditative moments in your daily life. You don't have to set aside hours of time. If you can, that may be helpful. If not, find short bits of time and make use of them each day. Meditation will help you become more clear and focused when you are engaged in those other activities that demand your conscious attention.

Meditation Goals

If your meditation goals go beyond relaxation, then you will want to experiment a bit to find methods that help you to achieve those goals. Don't get me wrong, relaxation is an admirable goal in our stressful modern lives. In fact, it is essential to physical and emotional health. Still, you may have other goals for your meditation.

Insight

Insight is a time-honored goal of meditation. Eastern adepts and Western monks and nuns have spent years in meditation or retreat in order to discover their connection to the universal plan. Your personal goals are just as important to you.

I will relate a story told to me by an elderly Episcopal priest. He had been a priest all his adult life. During the Lenten season he had undertaken a forty-day retreat, something most of us will never do. He had devoted his life to understanding the nature of God and to helping others. In a conversation with me concerning how we demonstrate our love of God and what we feel we owe God, he said, "You know, Stephanie, I have been a priest for over sixty-five years, and in these past weeks on retreat I have only now learned something about Him. God does not put us on Earth just so that we can love Him. He puts us here so that He can love us." This simple statement changed my life. Since that conversation I have often remembered this, and I have occasionally shared it with people who seemed to need reassurance that we each are part of a larger spiritual plan.

Now, we are not all priests or monks and we cannot all go on extended meditation retreats. What we *can* do is take the moments we have to calm our minds. Then we can perceive our place in the universal plan more clearly. You may connect through the Goddess, through multiple gods, through vibrational methods, through scientific investigation, or whatever means suits you. You can devote as much time as you wish to your meditation goals. Personally, I have found that more is not necessarily better, but some is necessary. The pace of my life could easily prevent me from having the time to write, for example. I can always find something else to do. Brief moments of quiet allow me to formulate and reorganize my thoughts. Then I can sit down and put the words together.

When you have a complex problem in the work environment, you need to get away from it to get a different perspective and to let the details sort themselves out in a way that points to a solution. Meditation provides one means of this. Sometimes a walk around the block is enough to accomplish this task.

Regarding the practice of meditation, Khenpo Karthar Rinpoche has written:

> Many people expect the result of meditation to come in a short space of time, overnight, so to speak, but this is not possible. It is a process of development wherein consistency is the key. If we practice every day, regularly, even for a short period of time, that will add to our development.[1]

Whatever your meditation goals, you can begin with just the simple act of sitting down and trying it. You don't need any fancy equipment or clothing and you need not revolutionize your daily schedule. Eventually you may want to find a teacher or attend workshops, but for now all you have to do is begin.

---

1. Karthar Rinpoche, *Transforming*, 5.

beginning to meditate

Read through the exercise, then close the book.

1. Sitting comfortably with your hands in your lap, or standing in a quiet spot, look at the cover of this book.

2. Relax your eyes and simply look.

3. Allow your attention to examine the details of the book's cover.

4. Continue doing this until you see something that catches your attention.

5. Then focus on why it caught your attention. Was it the color, the shape, the texture?

6. Refocus on the book's cover, and continue for a few moments.

7. Does something else arise to take your attention?

8. Notice any connections you make between the book's cover and your personal experience as you do this exercise.

Whatever arises for you is a bit of insight. It may not be the most profound insight you will ever experience, but it is insight. In the moments when we are not totally focused on the outer environment, or when we have a gap in our thought process, we allow insight to pop into our minds.

You don't need a huge gap, just a relaxed state and attention to the meditation process.

The simple act of altering your focus can place you in a slightly altered state of mind. In fact, we alter our states of mind every moment of our waking (and sleeping) life. We are constantly processing information, relating it to what we already know, and storing it for future use. Usually we are not conscious of the process, but we enter an altered state from moment to moment to moment.

The next chapter introduces a few meditation postures and other meditation tips.

2

Getting Ready
to Meditate

Shakyamuni Buddha said in the sutras, "The essence of the Dharma is taming the mind." He said further, "In a quiet, solitary place, on a comfortable meditation mat and cushion, you should sit in the proper meditation posture, your back erect, maintaining the correct position of the body, and engage in the practice of samadhi."

Khenpo Karthar Rinpoche
Dharma Paths

ALTHOUGH SOME PEOPLE meditate while engaging in another activity such as walking, most meditation involves sitting still. In the process of remaining physically still and focusing the mind, we are able to still the complex physical and mental activities that keep us busy all the time. Traditional Hindu and Buddhist meditations involve specific postures, or poses, that are believed to assist in

calming the mind. Buddhist and Hindu paintings show figures seated in a variety of postures, most frequently full
lotus and the Burmese posture. Some statues and paintings
show the figure seated on a platform with one leg extended
downward, while the other is bent close to the body with
the sole of the foot against the opposite thigh. From the
variety of artistic depictions, it seems evident that each
Buddha or teacher had a preferred style. They probably
arrived at this preference through trial and error, much as
you are about to do. There are as many positions for the
arms as there are for the legs and feet. Here again, you want
to find something that is comfortable for you. First, let's
consider the meditation environment.

The Meditation Setting

There are a number of things you can do to create a good
setting for meditation without spending a lot of money or
changing your lifestyle.

- Choose a spot that is conducive to quieting your mind.
  There will always be ambient noise, but you can turn
  off the television, radio, or stereo. Your eye can always
  find a place to direct its attention, but simple furniture
  and decorations are helpful.

- Arrange a table with flowers, pictures, or other objects
  that are meaningful to you. This sets the stage for meditation, and helps you cultivate a space in the environment that supports and reflects the space you develop
  within yourself.

- If you are grabbing a few minutes out of a busy day, carry something with you that you associate with your meditative state. It can be anything that helps you relax more quickly and easily.

- Identify a place in your body where you feel safe and relaxed during meditation. Focus your mind there for a few moments to center yourself.

For more on creating a meditation space, see chapter 21.

Clothing

Loose, comfortable clothing aids the meditation experience. Most practices include the removal of shoes, although you can keep them on to meditate when seated on a chair. Consider the temperature of the room as you prepare to meditate. Even on rather warm days you may find that after you have been seated quietly for a while, you become a bit cold. Layers of clothing, and perhaps a light shawl, provide you with the choice to add or remove garments to maintain your comfort zone.

As you gain experience, you will find that certain clothing works best for you. You may want to purchase specific clothes for meditation. Some people find that different colored fabrics have different effects on the meditation itself. Generally you will want to avoid itchy, scratchy fabric, materials that rustle when you move, and fabrics that do not "breathe." Clothing should not bind or inhibit circulation as you are sitting.

Choosing Your Meditation Posture

In the last chapter I mentioned that one positive outcome of meditation is muscle relaxation. For this outcome to occur, we each need to find a posture that we can assume and hold for the duration of the meditation period. Some postures will feel more relaxing than others. Many people will never be able to manage postures like full and half lotus. For us there are other possibilities. I will describe several traditional meditation postures, and you can try each one. If you find it uncomfortable, go on to a different one until you find something you can manage fairly easily. You may find that, after meditating for a while, you are able to assume a more difficult pose. Keep in mind that the goal is not to look a certain way, but to achieve a relaxed state of body and mind. Also remember to be careful when standing up. You may find that your leg or foot is "asleep," and will not support you without conscious effort.

Lotus Posture

Seat yourself on the floor or on a thin pad. Place your left foot on your right thigh, with the sole of the foot turned up or slightly up. Then place the right foot in a similar position on the left thigh. Your thighs and knees should be on the floor. Straighten your back, and place your hands on your thighs or knees. Some people extend the arms straight, rest the back of the wrists or hands on the knees, and form a circle with the thumbs and forefingers while the other fingers are extended. Another position is to have the hands resting together close to the body, with the

Figure 1. Lotus.

backs of the fingers of each hand touching the other, or with the fingers of one hand over the other and the thumb tips touching each other.

Half Lotus Posture

This posture is like full lotus, except that only one foot is on the opposite thigh, and the other foot is resting on the floor.

Seiza

This is a kneeling posture that involves sitting on the ankles. You can also use a thick round cushion called a *zafu* or a low bench for support. If you're using a bench,

Figure 2. Half lotus.

Figure 3. Seiza.

Figure 4. Cross-legged.

put your feet underneath it, and your knees on the floor or *zabuton* (large square floor cushion). Place your hands on your thighs. A hand position often used when sitting seiza is to interlock the fingers so they are inside your palms, then extend the forefingers so they are touching, and place the thumbs together. The hands then are allowed to rest on the thighs. You can also be kneeling directly on the floor in this posture. At first this may be very uncomfortable, but over time your ankles stretch and it is not so bad.

Sitting Cross-legged

Some people can sit cross-legged on a thin pad or directly on the floor. For those of us who find this uncomfortable, a cushion called a *gomden* has been designed. This is a very firm six-inch-high cushion. You can also use a zafu or a crescent-shaped cushion. You sit on the cushion with your back vertical and straight, and cross your legs in front of you on the floor. I like something to pad my ankles a bit. Then rock from side to side to settle into the cushion, and place your hands, palms down, on your thighs. Your upper arms should hang just about vertically. Spread your fingers comfortably, or use some other comfortable hand position. Your hands should rest in one place without slipping around.

Burmese Pose

This posture, and variations of it, are even more comfortable than the cross-legged posture. You sit on the zafu or other cushion, back straight and vertical. This time, instead of crossing your legs, you rest one foot ahead of or behind the other. This way there is no pressure from the leg on top. Rock from side to side to settle in, and choose a hand position that suits you.

Corpse Pose

No, this is not a joke. There is such a pose. You may find this one easier if you fold a blanket to lie on. Beds are generally too soft and too conducive to sleep. Recline on your back with your legs and feet comfortably together. You may want to support your lower back with a rolled-up towel or small pillow. Rest your arms and hands at your sides. Rest your head comfortably on the blanket. Close your eyes, but remain awake.

Figure 5. Burmese.

Eyes Open or Closed?

Different meditation techniques allow for one or the other. Closing your eyes will allow you to shut out the visual images in your environment, but it can be a strain to keep your eyes closed comfortably. Another drawback of closing your eyes is that you may tend to fall asleep. It is usually easy to have your eyes open, gazing downward at a point about six feet in front of you on the floor. Your eyes rest in such a position so that you don't have to work to keep them closed or fully open.

29

Tips for Making Your Meditation More Comfortable

- When you first sit down, rock on your chair or cushion from side to side. This firms your buttocks and creates a solid base. It also helps to position the intestines. Try this and notice that your abdomen feels more settled and comfortable.

- Next push your belly out, relax, and sit back a bit. This helps to achieve an erect posture and avoid slumping or leaning forward.

- Instead of focusing sharply, relax your eyes. When you do this you may notice that an object close to you seems to become double. If your focus is about six feet in front of you and slightly downward, you may notice the edges of patterns blur a little.

- Touch your tongue to the roof of your mouth. This helps to lessen the flow of saliva, and it keeps the tongue from moving around.

- Allow your chin to drop a little bit toward the throat. This relaxes the jaw and face muscles.

_____exercise

sitting down

If you have meditated before, this exercise may be unnecessary. If you have not, be gentle with your body as you try these different postures.

1. Read the instructions for each posture again.

2. Try each one to see if you can do it.

3. Choose one or two that are comfortable.

4. Use these throughout the other exercises in the book.

But It Hurts to Sit Still

Unless you are very flexible, you will find that sitting meditation places stress on joints and muscles, which causes some degree of pain. You may find that your leg or foot goes to sleep, and then tingles painfully when you move. Your back gets tired, and your knees hurt from sitting cross-legged. As with any other activity, you have to train your body to meditate. It's not just a mental activity. As with any other activity, each day you meditate you will find that your back gets stronger, your knees become more flexible, and your foot doesn't go to sleep as much.

If you meditate for just a few minutes, you may not experience physical discomfort. If you meditate for longer periods, you may want to get up and walk around a bit in the middle of your meditation time. During meditation retreats, each hour of sitting is broken up with a few minutes of walking meditation.

We can endure pain when we are playing a game or learning a skill. Many people go to the gym and work out to the point of pain in order to give themselves healthier bodies. The same is true of meditation. A little pain will distract you in the beginning, but it does not detract from the end benefits for both body and mind.

Any time you are working with your mind, some emotional response is likely. How often do you shy away from an activity because it is as emotionally straining as it is physical? Do you choose to engage in those activities where you excel, and retreat from areas where you can only achieve adequate, or even poor, results? In meditation the results are the results—nothing more and nothing less. There are no fixed goals, and there is no direct path. You may say you want to learn to relax. You find you can relax your muscles but not your mind, or vice versa. One day you lower your pulse and blood pressure, another you don't. What meditation gives you is a set of opportunities:

- To pay attention to your own mind.

- To develop a friendly relationship with yourself.

- To engage yourself at the intuitive level.

- To allow insight to arise.

_____**s u m m a r y**

Your meditation space need not be elaborately furnished. What helps is to have an orderly, quiet place and comfortable clothing. Next, you figure out a comfortable posture. Then you sit or lie still.

Now that you have considered a variety of ways to sit, the next chapter considers two elements of meditation—concentration and awareness.

3

Concentration
and Awareness

*Know your own mind. Train yourself to think what you
wish to think; be what you wish to be.*

Ernest Holmes
The Science of Mind

THERE ARE TWO factors involved in meditation:
concentration (focus) and awareness (mindfulness of your
focus and your immediate environment). These same two
factors are involved in all successful activities. If you can
concentrate on the task at hand, and if you can bring your
total awareness to the subject, then you will be more successful. You can observe concentration and mindfulness
going on around you all the time.

noticing mindfulness in others

Recall a time when you were watching an infant or small child at play. If you can't recall such a time, then go somewhere and watch a child for a while. As a courtesy, ask the parents or adult supervisor for permission to observe.

1. Notice what the child does. Watch the physical movements, the facial expressions, and the sounds the child makes.

2. Notice that while the child is focused, not much else seems to matter. The child's attention is fully engaged. Child development experts have noted that even children with ADHD can spend hours on projects that capture their attention.

3. Then notice when the child is distracted. What happens? Does the child go on to something else? Does his or her attention return to the earlier focus of attention? What does this tell you about how the child is perceiving the environment?

Children make great teachers. They seem capable of addressing one issue at a time. They are also able to let it go in favor of the next thing. We can learn a lot about how to be present in the world from this simple exercise.

Once you engage in meditation each day, what kinds of outcomes can you expect? While you may have one or more specific reasons to begin meditating, you will find that you get a wide variety of results. A few of them are listed here.

- **Ability to focus your attention narrowly on one thing at a time.** This capacity has value in everything you do. From tying your shoes quickly to preparing a seven-course meal, attention to the details is necessary. The child brings everything to her observation of an ant crossing the patio, slipping between the stones, only to emerge again. You have the most ecstatic experience of sex when you clear your mind of all distractions. Meditation helps you to develop and maintain focus.

- **Awareness.** Understanding what you perceive is also essential in everyday life. If you hear a sudden noise, knowing the difference between a branch hitting the roof and a burglar breaking in is helpful. Knowing your position in a dark room helps you move toward the light switch. Knowing that you have just awakened from a dream helps you put the dream experience in the context of your waking life. Meditation aids the development of simple awareness.

- **Awareness of distractions.** Often we don't know to what we are truly paying attention. Have you ever had the experience of driving along, and suddenly you were much farther down the road than the last time you looked? You were thinking about something else and failed to experience the trip. Perhaps you were once so hungry that you didn't take the time to experience the taste of your food. Where did your mind take you?

- **Remaining fully present.** A great deal of suffering has to do with the inability to remain fully present. We desperately need to be somewhere else in order to avoid the pain, but this strategy actually causes greater suffering. We usually have to return to the pain sooner or later to resolve it. When we play games, we often continue to play well past the comfort level into pain. We ache, and yet we continue to play because we find the game enjoyable. Khenpo Karthar Rinpoche has written, "Why could we not cheerfully handle other sorts of pain? We certainly have the ability."[1] We could just as well apply this tactic to any pain we experience. By cultivating focus and awareness, we face emotional pain and deal with it at once, instead of ignoring it and delaying resolution. It is true that not all pain goes away simply by paying attention. However, suffering is lessened when we understand the nature of physical, mental, emotional, and even spiritual pain.

Development of Awareness

Part of learning any new skill is an awareness of the goal and what is involved in getting there. Meditation is no different. So far we have seen that awareness is a potential outcome of meditation, and that concentration is involved in the process. What can we do to enhance the development of awareness? We simply pay attention to whatever happens during meditation.

---

1. Karthar Rinpoche, *Transforming*, 9.

Suppose your meditation method is to gaze at the flame of a candle. You find it is easy to focus on the flame. You settle into this task quickly. Soon you find your mind wandering to an itch on your knee. You come back to your awareness of the flame, but only after you scratch the itch. You then perceive that the color and intensity of what you see around the flame changes. When you blink, it changes again. You see wax dripping. You begin to sense the heat of the candle, even though it is several feet away from you. You come back to your awareness of the flame. You may even give up at this point, frustrated with this simple task.

You have not maintained steady awareness of the flame, even though that is your goal, and even though you were able to do it for a few moments at the outset. Why is maintaining this level of awareness so difficult? When we consider the myriad levels of experience involved in a simple task, the answer makes a lot of sense. We are complex physical beings designed to survive in a relatively hostile environment. The senses we use to understand what is happening around us do not simply switch off when we decide to concentrate. They keep right on working, and so does the mind. Thoughts arise all the time, whether we're awake or asleep. We can't easily shut them off.

Yet we know that daily meditation can calm nerves, lower blood pressure, and so on. We know change occurs as soon as we begin. The following exercise, taken from the master's thesis of a dance therapy student, illustrates one way to engage in the experience of distraction in order to fully understand the richness of trained attention.

paying attention

As you are reading this paper, these very words, bring your attention to your hands holding or touching the paper. As you do this,

1. Notice the information you receive, about the texture of the paper, the weight, etc.

2. Become aware of your hands and fingertips themselves.

3. Open your awareness to your environment: the chair you are sitting on, the room, the temperature in the room, to sounds, smells, etc.

4. Take some time to stay with this exercise.[2]

In this exercise you are intentionally opening your mind to whatever you can experience. By staying with the immediate experience, you can identify distinct senses and how they play into your thoughts about the exercise, the words, the paper, the environment. You may begin to discover that you have some feelings concerning the exercise. As you stay with the process, you cultivate a friendly or curious attitude toward the process.

Three outcomes of developing awareness are unconditional positive regard, insight, and intuition. These topics will be discussed in detail in the following chapters, but I am including information about them here because these

---

2. Wenger, "The Training of Attention," 6.

three kinds of knowledge and appreciation are central themes in most meditation practices.

Unconditional Positive Regard

The term *unconditional positive regard*, taken from humanistic and transpersonal psychology, simply means remaining aware of yourself (or of another person) without making any judgments. This is actually difficult to accomplish. We continually find small flaws or faults in ourselves, in other people, or in the process of life. When we are engaged in such judgment, we are certainly not paying full attention to what is happening in the moment, and we are probably creating the potential for suffering. After all, if we judge something as bad, then we dislike having to deal with it. Therefore we may suffer whenever we have to deal with it. Unconditional positive regard allows us to perceive something without evaluating it.

Insight and Intuition

As you gain skill in focusing your attention, you begin to experience whole periods of time when you are not distracted by constant thoughts. In these moments or gaps you experience just being yourself. Then your intuition can speak to you. There has to be a quiet moment for most of us, or we simply can't hear the quiet intuitive voice.

Insight resolves a question or reveals a solution to a problem. It can involve anything you are working on in the present. There is an "Aha!" quality to insight when the pieces of a puzzle suddenly fit together. The Episcopal priest's example of insight in the first chapter illustrates how insight arises during or after meditation.

You will recognize intuition because it is bright, shiny, loud, and clear. It can be ordinary or very strange. You may not associate the content of your intuition with anyone or anything in particular. On the other hand, you may know exactly what to do with information that relates to the future in some way.

If you are meditating and an idea arises so forcefully that you cannot distract yourself, you may want to write a few notes to yourself about it. Then you can return to your meditation. Later you can review your notes and apply the information to your daily activities, your work, or whatever. At first every thought may seem important and your meditation note pad may be full, but with a bit of practice you will be able to isolate insights that are meaningful to your problem-solving process and you may write less.

summary

If these results seem unattainable, recall the first exercise in chapter 1 in which you looked at the cover of this book. Within just a moment or two you experienced the capacity to see something in a new way. With just a few minutes of meditation each day you can cultivate concentration and awareness too.

In the next chapter, we consider you. There, we look at ways to develop a positive attitude toward meditation.

4

Be Kind to Yourself

What we need to experience, and what we can experience, is a saner and gentler state of mind. This experience is not found in something outside of us. . . . We must work with our own minds, with our own abilities, in order to have peaceful, rich minds.

Khenpo Karthar Rinpoche
*Transforming Mental Afflictions
and Other Selected Teachings*

YOU HAVE BEEN meditating now for a few days or weeks. You think you are getting the hang of it—you relax, breathe, and focus. Suddenly you notice that your thinking is all over the place. You focus for one or two breaths, and then you are mentally in the kitchen, in the car, following your children or friends around—you are doing everything *but* focusing. You begin to wonder why you can't do this simple meditation thing.

Now would be a good time to congratulate yourself for meditating exactly the way you are supposed to! Part of the practice of meditation is allowing to arise whatever wants or needs to arise. When you are busy with all your daily tasks, you don't leave much time for this to happen. You have thoughts every moment, but they are not so much coming from deep within you as just occurring one after the other in the course of problem solving.

Develop an unconditional positive regard for these thoughts that keep popping into your meditation. These are your very own thoughts. No one is putting them into your mind. These thoughts reveal a great deal about how your mind works, and as such are valuable tools for achieving deeper relaxation, clearing out old business, and making room for something new to develop. They show you the nature of your mental habits. You can't change a habit until you understand its purpose, and meditation gives you plenty of opportunities to experience your habitual thinking processes.

Another great value of random thoughts that arise in meditation is that they point to little centers or complexes of emotional and mental energy. Such complexes, when rigid or distorted, are called neuroses. Neurotic thought patterns lead to neurotic behaviors that cause friction within your personality and in relationships with others. The fact that you have thoughts arising when you meditate indicates that you are approaching a clearer understanding of the mental distortions that limit your life in some way.

All behaviors began as an initial response to a need or desire. While you are busy trying to resolve the mental processes you meet in meditation, remember that at some time in the past these behaviors had a positive purpose. In fact, most of our behaviors have a positive intention behind them, or had positive value in the past. We may have outgrown the need for a particular response without discarding the habit. Examining the thoughts that lead to a particular behavior reflects your capacity to pay attention to yourself. You honor your own choices and behaviors when you do this; you indicate unconditional positive regard for yourself. The only place you can begin, when meditating, is with your own mind. Whatever is there, you will get a chance to pay attention to it. You will "see" images, "hear" voices, experience physical sensations, and perceive emotional responses. Whatever you experience, it is you. You probably have all too few moments when you are able to simply be yourself. Now that you have the opportunity, be compassionate with yourself—even when you are mentally criticizing your own meditation technique!

---

exercise

being gentle with your thoughts

Begin your meditation by getting comfortable. Bring a pencil and paper with you in case you want to make a note about anything.

1. As you begin to focus your mind, observe how your body relaxes itself. You may notice your breathing is slower. Certain muscle groups release their tension.

2. As stray ideas enter your thoughts, notice them, and let them pass through.

3. Refocus yourself.

4. Perhaps an especially irritating idea arises. Just notice it and let it pass through. If an idea simply won't go away, write one or two sentences about the idea.

5. Then return to your meditation. Do this for at least ten minutes.

How many ideas did you feel compelled to record? Was there much that seemed vitally important? Did some of the thoughts just pass on by without making much of an impression? Did the same thought come up again and again? By paying attention in this way—writing down whatever thought was compelling enough to stick with you—you are acknowledging your own mental process. There is no criticism here, as there is no critic. You are simply observing your own mental function.

I find that in meditation I may remember something I have to pick up at the store. By writing it down, I can let go of the worry that I may forget. Sometimes the image of a friend sticks in my mind. If I write down the name, I will remember to call or write. If a memory of something happy, angry, or sad arises, a sentence can help me acknowledge that bit of my history. I find that after a while, there are fewer thoughts that seem so compelling, and those few that are take on greater significance. While not much will have changed in my work and social life, I have experienced a renewed relationship with myself in which I have offered myself respect and attention.

Khenpo Karthar Rinpoche wrote the following about the meaning of meditation:

> Meditation practice is very important in anyone's daily life. Meditation means to apply the appropriate techniques to cultivate a gentler, calmer mind. It also refers to the process of getting used to this sane state of mind.[1]

You may find that this more relaxed, self-respecting state of mind is a refreshing change. Think about it: why should you beat yourself up over every little thing that happens? You are doing the best you can all the time. Besides, other people are critical enough of your decisions, actions, and results. When you take the time to regard yourself unconditionally and positively in meditation, you are offering yourself a gift without price.

_____exercise

noticing thoughts

This exercise can be done anytime. You just need a few minutes. You can do this instead of reading a magazine in a reception area when you are waiting to be called for an appointment. If there are other people around, you may want to close your eyes. This provides a signal that you are

---

1. Karthar Rinpoche, *Transforming*, 8.

not interested in talking. If you are alone, you can adopt your usual meditation pose.

1. Begin your meditation as usual.

2. Notice the first thought that occurs to you.

3. Instead of letting it go, focus on the thought for a moment. Evaluate it, or reword it in your mind.

4. Then go back to your meditation, with the intention of finding more information about that thought.

5. Notice the next thought. Compare it to the first one. Do they seem related? If not, imagine a connection between them, and go back to your meditation.

6. Notice the next thought, and so on.

If there is a goal here, it is to notice your thoughts without judgment. In this exercise, the thoughts become the focus. You may be curious about how the thoughts relate to each other, but you don't need to struggle to establish connections. Just notice that the thoughts arise one after the other. When you are finished, you will often find that your first thought has connections to other thoughts; it came up by itself and now fits into a broader picture. This meditation process could be called *reverie*. You simply allow thoughts to come to you, and then you examine them with curiosity.

The last exercise here at the end of the chapter suggests the possibility of identifying a thought or problem, and then allowing your mind to have another thought, with no pressure to resolve anything. This is a problem-solving technique that can become part of your daily routine.

I find that the act of straightening my desk is a sort of meditation; each paper, book, or file acts as an arising thought. As I put things away and straighten the stacks of paper, my mind moves freely from one thing to the next without expecting any particular associations. When I am finished, I am then able to go back to a task with a clear mind. By doing this, I have been kind to myself in several ways. I have made my office more attractive, I have rediscovered items that were (seemingly) lost, I have arranged my working materials so I can find them in the future, and I have given myself a five- or ten-minute break from grand-scale problem solving by solving little organizational problems. Finally, I have provided myself with a successful outcome: I have made my surroundings more comfortable.

The next chapter presents a traditional style of meditation called *Shamata*, or *Shinay*.

5

Getting Past
the First Step

*One has to taste for oneself and find out if the thing is gen-
uine, or helpful, but before discarding it one has to go a little bit further, so that at least one gets first hand experience
of the preliminary stage.*

Chogyam Trungpa Rinpoche
Meditation in Action

YOU ARE ON the path toward regular meditation, and you find you need something a bit more systematic. You are getting the idea of things, and you want to
shape your meditation. This chapter introduces a popular
method of meditation. *Shamata*, a Sanskrit word, is *Shinay*
in Tibetan. *Shi* means "peace" or "pacification"; the lessen-
ing of the power of continuous thought. *Nay* means "to
abide"; by developing tranquility, we let the mind rest on a

chosen subject or focus. So tranquility meditation leads to the development of abiding peace of mind.

Tranquility meditation shares qualities with other meditation practices. In fact, I can think of no meditative practice that does not result in greater peace of mind. This peace comes partly from conscious relaxation. It also derives from accepting whatever thoughts we have, instead of repressing or rejecting them. It comes from paying total attention to ourselves for a few minutes each day, with no thought for the rest of the day.

exercise

tranquility meditation

1. Sit comfortably on the floor, on a cushion, or in a chair. Sit upright, but do not strain to do so. Sitting upright allows you to breathe properly.

2. Place your hands lightly on your thighs. Your arms should not feel any stress. Your elbows will be close to your torso.

3. Focus your eyes about six feet in front of you, looking down toward the floor. Again, find a focus point that is easy to maintain without stress.

4. Now pay attention to your breath. Notice how it feels to breathe in and out. Follow your breath out, almost as though you can see the movement of the air.

5. You will naturally breathe in again. Then follow the breath out.

6. As you do this, thoughts will occur naturally. The idea of the meditation is to recognize the thoughts, and then return to following your breath.

7. Label the thoughts "thinking," check the comfort of your posture, and then follow the breath again.

This single-pointed meditation can have an object—such as a candle—for its focus. With practice, you will find that you cease to stare at your focal point, and your eyes become relaxed and perhaps slightly defocused.

You will find that this meditation is simple, but not necessarily easy. You will sit, breathe, and find that myriad thoughts come to you. You will squirm to get more comfortable. This meditation requires patience, and patience is one of the key qualities you develop along the way. Just as developing skill at a sport takes effort and patience, learning to sit still—still in mind and body—requires time. As your meditation skill increases, you will find you are more patient with other people in your daily activities. This is because you are able to bring your full attention to those individuals.

Focus of Attention

There needs to be a focus. It can be on a visual point, an object, or on the breath. If breath is your focus, you want to allow each breath to occur naturally. Inhale and feel the breath going in. When you exhale, feel the breath going out into the space around you. By following both the inward and outward breath, you are able to maintain a steady focus. After a few breaths, your focus will be on the breathing process, and awareness of outer circumstances will be greatly reduced.

What to Expect

The mind is incredibly busy with distracting thoughts. You may be astonished at how much activity there is. The thoughts at first seem random and scattered—they are "bouncing off the walls."

The mind moves into a state of one-way flow. As you settle down, you find your thoughts take on a more consistent direction. There is an almost constant flow, but it goes in a general direction—more like a stream flowing downhill. There are a few rocks and a few bends, but the flow goes in one general direction.

After a while the thoughts do not distract you from the focus of your attention. This is a fairly high level of achievement. You may feel this for a few minutes and then revert back to the "busy-mind" stage or the "flowing" stage. Still, you have glimpsed a state of peace in which you can be fully engaged in the meditation while acknowledging that thoughts are continuously occurring.

Eventually your mind will quiet as soon as you sit down, or within only a few moments. This is a result of practice and familiarity. You slip into a quiet, comfortable, familiar space and are able to remain there throughout your meditation.

Some days you will not come close to this mental state. This can be frustrating, as you expect consistent progress.

This intermittent interruption in your meditation represents its own kind of progress. As you extend your meditation practice, you will develop even greater compassion for your not-so-meditative days.

To understand this style of meditation, you need to continue until you get the experience of being able to calm the mind as soon as you begin the meditation. The simple act of altering your focus can place you in a slightly altered state of mind. Yet it is important not to expect or demand this relaxed state of yourself. Thus, you should go with whatever you get each time you meditate, while focusing on the object or the breath.

There are two main obstacles to meditation, and there are ways to work with both of them.

1. You may experience a weak feeling, or even fall asleep. Such a state is unlikely to produce much benefit, yet it is what you are feeling, and can be accepted as part of you. To remedy sleepiness or weakness, raise your level of attention to the meditation—to how you are sitting, how you are breathing, how you perceive the object. Correct your posture by sitting a bit straighter or firmer. Look up at the sky or the ceiling. Flex a few muscles. If you won't disturb other people's meditation, get up and walk a bit, paying direct attention to how you move.

   You may also want to visualize the breath as containing white light. Imagine it spreading through your body as you inhale. As you exhale, your breath is white light that floats up and dissolves in space.

2. Excitement is another possible response. This can be caused by compelling thoughts that arise, or by distractions in the immediate environment. Either of these keep you from settling into the meditation. To alleviate excitement, try diverting your gaze a bit downward, or even closing your eyes for a few minutes. Relax your posture a bit, then straighten again. You may want to roll your shoulders to relax the muscles. Visualize that you exhale blue, indigo, or black light and imagine the darkness settling into the ground. Then breathe in the same color of light so that it pervades your body with calming darkness.

Remember, the key to meditation practice is to do some each day. Find a time that works for you, and try to sit down at that time. At first you may want to experiment to find a time that works for you consistently. You also will find that during the day you have moments when you can relax and meditate. You don't have to meditate at the same time each day, but you may find that you drift into a regular schedule without effort.

Benefits of Shamata Practice for the Beginner

- You will just become happier. It is that simple. You will worry less. You will have fewer neurotic thoughts. You will have less fear. You will begin to recognize that the state of your mind is based on internal, not external, conditions.

- You learn to focus. In shamata meditation, distractions occur. As you continue meditation, you are less subject to distraction, and you maintain calmness. By learning to maintain clear focus on whatever task you are doing, you will extend this skill to other activities. You will consequently be able to get more accomplished.

- Because you are happier and more productive, you will be easier to get along with. People will be more confident in your abilities because you are—you don't just seem to be, you are—more stable.

- You are able to hold your position mentally, physically, or emotionally. You are like a cube resting on the ground—you don't tip easily.

- When you do have one of those less attractive emotions come over you, you are able to go with it. For example, you do anger while you are angry, instead of pushing the feeling away. By doing this you are then able to go on to the next thing without carrying a less constructive feeling around with you.

s u m m a r y

When you meditate, you listen to yourself, you experience yourself, and you work with yourself. This is the most important goal of your meditation. All other beneficial results come about because you are working with yourself.

Dharma means "work." While I don't think of meditation as work any more, I used to have to work at it pretty hard. The following is what Khenpo Karthar says about the dharma:

> If you do not speak Tibetan, you have not missed much. You have your own language. On the other hand, if you do not know the dharma, you are missing a great deal.[1]

The rest of this book suggests additional facets of meditation, and additional meditative practices that may satisfy your individual needs more fully. The next chapter considers the practice of insight meditation, as insight is a natural outgrowth of tranquility meditation.

---

1. Karthar Rinpoche, *Transforming*, 162.

6

Experiencing Insight and Intuition

People tend to make a very sharp distinction between spiritual life and everyday life. They will label a man as "worldly" or "spiritual" and they generally make a hard and fast division between the two.

Chogyam Trungpa Rinpoche
Meditation in Action

IN THE TWENTY-FIRST century there is a profound need to overcome the apparent gap between worldliness and spirituality. It is essential to integrate our physical, emotional, mental, and spiritual lives in meaningful ways. We are involved in an incredibly fast-paced social and economic system. In many cases, we are moving forward without completing tasks, and thus we feel a sense of incompleteness pervading our lives. Sadness and a sense of loss are the inevitable results of such an incomplete life.

Many people are searching for reasons for the events and feelings we experience; they are searching for the answers to the existential questions that surround us.

Each person has a seed within that is the potential he or she was born with. It can be a lust for power, violence, an intellectual thirst, a profound desire for love—it can be anything that an individual wants and truly believes.[1] Along with the inherent seed there is a voice, which is the inner spirit. This daimon is always there, it never leaves, and it sometimes pushes each of us in the direction we must take. The voice may be quiet sometimes, or it may virtually shout at us to make changes. It applauds, cajoles, nudges, and teases. It may even resort to trickery to get us to change. Insight meditation is one way to pay direct attention to the inner voice.

exercise

vipassana, or insight meditation

1. The posture is the same as for tranquility meditation. Your eyes are not focused on the floor, but directed straight ahead into the distance. This will include your peripheral vision.

2. As you breathe, notice whatever enters your attention visually. Remember the exercise with the book cover? That focused on one object. Now you are simply experiencing whatever you can see.

1. Trungpa Rinpoche, *Meditation in Action*, 20–21.

3. Don't become fascinated with what you see. Simply remain aware. You will find that your mind wanders from one thing to the next: the texture of the carpet, the color of the wall, the light coming in the window, the picture on the wall, the leg of a chair—whatever is there to be seen.

This meditation helps you to become aware of your surroundings, and to appreciate the detail and richness around you. We seldom take the time to view the world in this kind of intense way. As you learn to do this, you will find that your day-to-day environment seems brighter and more interesting.

Trungpa Rinpoche adds this about vipassana:

This basic form of meditation is concerned with trying to see what *is*. There are many variations on this form of meditation, but they are generally based on various techniques for opening oneself. The achievement of this kind of meditation is . . . what one might call "working meditation" or extrovert meditation, where skilful means and wisdom must be combined like the two wings of a bird. This is not a question of trying to retreat from the world.[2]

I remember a time when I was driving with my mother. We were being followed by other family members in a second vehicle. There had been a rainstorm, and I had been sharply focused on driving in the rain. My mother was looking out the window and said, "Look

---

2. Ibid., 52.

at that rainbow! It's glorious." I looked for a second, and went back to driving.

She continued to say how wonderful the rainbow was, that it was double, and even that it became a triple rainbow. I said I couldn't look, as I was driving.

My mother said, "Well, pull off on the shoulder, then." So I did. We got out of the car and just stood there looking at this incredible rainbow.

The other car pulled up behind us, and my brother said, "What's wrong?" It became clear that my mother and I were the only two who thought the rainbow was interesting enough to stop for on the interstate. It was difficult to explain why we thought it was so important to us. I think we ended up saying we were doing it because we could. I have never seen such a glorious rainbow again, and to this day I vividly remember that shared moment from over thirty years ago.

Meditation offers us the opportunity to stop the car and see—really see—the rainbow. An indirect benefit of meditation practice is that you will find more and more opportunities like my rainbow. You will find that you can take one or two minutes to look at a thing, or think a thought, or listen to a sound, and more fully engage your senses in the experience. You will be able to pay attention to everyday things more fully.

This attention, or concentration, is something we all engage in when we work and play. It is not something new. However, what *is* new is the development of a greater capacity to choose when and where to concentrate. When you are working on a problem for school or your job, you want to be able to shut out ambient distractions, and you have learned ways to do this. When you are learning a new task, you focus on the steps in the process to the exclusion of sensory input that does not aid learning this particular task. When you are deeply involved in a game, you may ignore signals of hunger for an extended period of time because you are more interested in the game.

Insight meditation trains the mind to voluntarily enter the state of concentration; then insight arises. This insight concerns what *is*. It concerns your personal mental activity, the obstacles to listening to the inner voice, and the obstacles to seeing what is right here and now. As you develop more meditative skill, you will be able to acknowledge and accept whatever negative thoughts are found within yourself. You will be able to work with them instead of denying them. You will use them as the earth in which you plant the seeds of insight.

Everything you have been in past lives and in the past during this lifetime comes together in the one point that is you now. The future opens up from this one point to all the possibilities that exist. By allowing yourself to consider all past possibilities, you open to future possibilities as well. The idea is to examine the past, but not sink into momentary urges that cause harm or pain. Meditation helps you consider past events and feelings and then let them go once you understand them.

You may be striving to achieve a more spiritual state of mind. To do this you must also to understand the other side of your being: the Shadow. Carl Jung developed the concept of the Shadow, a less conscious component of one's being. Without understanding the urges of this Shadow, it is difficult, if not impossible, to become an integrated personality. In insight meditation, you not only are distracted by thoughts concerning, for example, the past or facets of yourself that you dislike; you are also occasionally moved by insight into the way you have acted and why you are unwilling to accept those unattractive characteristics. The Shadow, according to Jung, can provide the information you need to achieve balance within your personality.

Each of us has a uniquely personal insight into the world. We are not like those twenty second-graders who are all supposed to gain insight into the meaning of certain words in the reading assignment for the day, or learn the value of certain addition and subtraction tasks. We have our own interpretations of whatever "words" come to us, and we are fully capable of adding two and two and arriving at our own answers. We are not limited by a linear, one-answer-fits-all kind of thinking.

You may find that some of the material presented here about insight fits pretty well with you, while other ideas are off the mark. Your insight into the practice itself may begin with the words in this book as you sort out what works for you and what can be left for another reader.

The following exercises may help you understand your Shadow side and how it works.

_____e x e r c i s e

meditating on the shadow

Think of something that you really dislike.

1. As you begin meditation, focus on this thing very closely.

2. Examine it in all its distasteful reality.

3. As you focus, notice what stray thoughts arise.

4. Notice any feeling that you feel, emotionally or in your body.

5. Really get into the badness of the thing you are examining.

6. As you do this, notice how your attitude toward the thing changes.

---
exercise

meditating on the lighter side

Think of something that you really like.

1. As you begin meditation, focus on this thing very closely.

2. Examine it in all its appealing reality.

3. As you focus, notice what stray thoughts arise.

4. Notice any feeling that you feel, emotionally or in your body.

5. Really get into the goodness of the thing you are examining.

6. As you do this, notice how your attitude toward the thing changes.

The results of these two exercises may surprise you. I find that when I really examine something that I dislike, something arises to show me that there is a positive mixed in with the negatives. The opposite is true of examining something I really like. The insight could be as simple as thinking, "Why am I spending valuable time looking so closely at this thing I really like?" It could be insight into how the light and dark play of shadows adds depth to an image.

_____s u m m a r y

Insight may elude you for a while. Patience is necessary to achieve results with insight meditation. You have learned so far to be generous with yourself, to accept whatever ideas come up as you meditate. You have learned something of the discipline of meditating each day for a few minutes, finding even a few minutes you can devote solely to yourself (another form of generosity). Now you have to keep doing what you are doing, even if it seems like nothing is happening.

The next chapter explores how meditation results in altered states of consciousness.

7

Altered States
of Consciousness

*Going into an altered state is nothing weird. You do it all
the time. The question is whether you use the altered state
to produce change.*

Richard Bandler and John Grinder
Frogs into Princes

IN THE SIXTIES, we thought an altered state of
mind was something induced by drugs. Not that drugs are
anything new; alcoholic beverages alter one's consciousness, and they have been around since about the beginning of recorded history or longer. Opiates have been used
for both medicinal and recreational purposes since the first
century or earlier. Coffee and chocolate alter the brain's
chemistry, and thus the state of consciousness. Some of us
are affected by changes in the weather.

With the introduction of Hinduism and Buddhism in the West, we have incorporated some of the basic principles of mind-altering practices into our daily language. We joke about good or bad karma (a Sanskrit term). When we say, "Give me space," oftentimes what we really mean is "Give me both the time and space I need to think."

Now, at the beginning of the twenty-first century, we alter our minds with television, the Internet, and electronic games. Using technology, we can enter a virtual reality and experience something very like the real deal. We use aromatherapy to soothe our bodies and minds. We use headphones to shut out ambient reality and to create a different one for ourselves. We have dozens of ways to tune in, tune out, and turn on.

Actually, we enter an altered state of consciousness very frequently. If I change the subject, first I enter an altered state, and then I induce you to do the same. Each time your attention wanders from one thing to the next, you enter an altered state. This is how we relate to the world—by changing the state of mind.

exercise

changing states of mind

1. Spend one minute thinking about just one thing.

Okay. Were you able to do that, or did your mind wander off the topic? For most of us, wandering off the topic is inevitable. On the other hand, if I had instructed, "Don't think about a red car," you might have found that you had numerous visions of red cars go through your mind: convertibles, hot little sports models, conservative cranberry-colored Crown Victorias, and so on. You may have wandered off the topic to fire trucks, pick-ups, and vans. You may have even had time to escape the red group and try a different color, but you probably would have stayed with cars and red. Odd, isn't it, that it is sometimes easier to do what you are told not to do?

Meditation is an altered state of mind too. Studies have shown that meditation alters the physical, mental, and emotional states of meditators. There are three central alterations that occur, and each has its own emotional quality.

1. Resting the body comes first. To meditate, you rest the body. Generally you sit still in a position that is not overly stressful. Some of us can sit in the lotus posture, with our legs crossed and our hands extended over the knees. Others of us will never be able to manage that, but we can sit relatively still. Getting situated occupies the mind, and we let go of some of the urgent questions and problems we were thinking about just a moment before.

2. Resting the mind is second. This is not so simple, but we can generally relax for a few minutes and let go of the pressing issues of our lives. We find that as we try to do this, we experience relaxation in the facial muscles. We close the eyes, perhaps, or let the skin on the forehead and cheeks sag just a little. The jaw

drops a bit. All this happens when we try to relax the mind.

3. Focusing the mind comes third. Once we are seated and relaxed, then the mind begins to wander. We now have to focus on something.

wandering thoughts

Find a nice place to sit for a few moments. Perhaps you are already sitting, in which case you don't even have to move.

1. Relax, put this book down, and just settle your mind into the exercise.

2. Without using any effort, simply pay attention to what you see, hear, smell, taste, and feel.

3. Pay attention to how your mind wanders from one thing to the next.

It is incredibly easy to be distracted as you try this exercise. In just thirty seconds I was aware of the crick in my back, the sound of the chair as I leaned back, the sound of an airplane going by, the fan in my computer, the feel of my hands resting in my lap, even the sensation as my eyelids closed.

Meditation Goal

One of the goals of most meditation practices is to alter your state of consciousness in a specific way. At first this seems nearly impossible. Your mind changes all right, but when you sit down and try to clear your mind, dozens of stray thoughts arise to plague the peace you are seeking. You can't seem to get to the desired state of peace.

It may be helpful to redefine what we mean by altered state of consciousness. Perhaps the definition is too narrow. Yes, we meditate in order to achieve a more peaceful, restful state of mind. The problem may be that we have defined this state without understanding what has to happen to get there. We may also have labeled other states of consciousness as being bad because they are not peaceful or restful.

We experience altered states of mind from moment to moment. Everything other than what we are thinking, feeling, or hoping for at this very moment is an altered state. Most medications cause an altered state. Coffee, alcohol, cigarettes, and chocolate all can alter our consciousness. Warm clothing, cool air, a bath, perfume—you name it—all create altered states.

If everything is an altered state of consciousness, then it shouldn't be too hard to achieve one. Just be open to anything and everything.

Now that we understand how easy it is to alter our state of consciousness, we can move toward an answer to the actual question: How do I learn to achieve a more relaxed, more peaceful state of mind? How do I dig around in all those possible altered states to find the ones that make me feel better, or lower my blood pressure, or enhance my compassion for others?

So far in this book you have learned a little bit about how people meditate, and you have looked into the mechanisms of concentration and awareness. You have learned that you must be kind to yourself first, and you have even seen how to get past the first step. You have entered the realm of sitting meditation, and as you sit, you begin to see what kinds of thoughts and feelings come to you. You begin to understand the altered states of mind that are typical in your life. This is because the thoughts that arise when you meditate are the same familiar thoughts, or kinds of thoughts, that you have all the time.

Perhaps you tend to make a list of the things you "ought" to be doing instead of meditating. Maybe your thoughts go to feelings about things that happened yesterday, last week, or twenty years ago. You may think about your parents, children, spouse, or friends. Work issues may come up again and again. Any problem you are trying to resolve may enter your mind in a variety of forms. If these things or things like them occur when you meditate, you can congratulate yourself for being completely normal. Welcome to the world of altered states!

Meditation is not actually about getting those thoughts to go away. After all, you have the kinds of thoughts you need each day in order to get your work done, prepare meals, or engage in social activities. You will want to be able to continue having those thoughts on an as-needed basis. What you want from meditation is to develop the skill of relaxing your mind so that you have greater control over how and when certain thoughts arise.

For example, when I was younger, I experienced the death of both of my parents. I grieved very hard for them. I thought about them all the time. I fretted over incidental slights—both things they did or did not do for me, and things I said or did that hurt them. I could hardly think of anything else, and when I did think about something else, I felt guilty for forgetting my parents. Needless to say, this general state of mind was very uncomfortable, and was not conducive to getting on with my life.

Some time after their deaths, I undertook learning about meditation. I sat, sometimes comfortably and sometimes not. Sometimes I was fairly peaceful, and sometimes I was not. I even attended meditation practices with my children. Gradually I found that I could usually attain a calmer state of mind within a few minutes.

Years passed.

When I heard that my father-in-law died suddenly, I immediately put my head down on my desk and cried. Not just a little. I did some serious crying for about two minutes. Then I tried to continue the phone conversation with my husband. He said, "That is exactly what I did when I got the call." Both of us cried intensely for a few minutes. Then we got on with what we needed to do about making plans—calmly. We weren't cheerful, but we were able to create a plan of action.

I let someone else drive me home that day. It was really nice to have a coworker in the car with whom I could chat about this and that so that I was distracted from the immediate problem.

What I found, as the days unfolded, was that I was able to focus on the best things about my father-in-law. He had spent a lot of time with us, driving into town for lunches and dinners, shopping for furnishings for our house, fixing little things that needed repair. Both my husband and I found that when we thought about him, we missed him, we were glad that his passing did not involve suffering, and we were at peace.

I believe that those years of meditation made the difference between second-guessing myself about the past and remembering the good things about a gentle man who had entered my life. Surprisingly, I found that I was also able to remember the good things about my own parents, and to set aside the presumed wrongs that may have occurred. I had changed the way thoughts arose in my mind! I had changed the pathways to include the positive, constructive, meaningful thoughts, and to avoid the pitfalls of negative and destructive ones.

Well, I still have the negative thoughts. They occur less frequently, and they stay with me for shorter periods of time. I am therefore more content with my life.

exercise

changing your pulse rate

Research has shown that individuals can raise or lower their blood pressure through physical activity. If you walk, jog, or run, you will increase your blood pressure. As you slow down, blood pressure falls back toward normal. You can manipulate your mental state in a similar way.

1. Assume your meditative posture and take a moment to relax. Take a few deep breaths. Feel the spots where your body meets the floor, cushion, or chair.

2. Notice your rate of breathing. Place your fingers on your throat and feel your pulse.

3. Now imagine yourself engaging in a vigorous activity. Perhaps you are running up a hill to catch up with your dog. Chase him around at the top of the hill. Imagine doing this until you begin to tire.

4. Place your fingers on your throat again. Even though you have not changed your physical position, you find that your pulse has increased. Just thinking about the chase sped up your heart.

5. Now imagine you have the dog on his leash. You start back down the hill. Instead of hurrying, you wander back and forth. He sniffs the plants for signs of rabbits and other small animals. You notice the color of the plants, the rocks, whatever is in your path. You may even pick up some small thing to examine. You feel the warmth of the sun on your back.

6. Place your fingers on your throat again. You will find that once again, without physically moving, your pulse has changed—it has come back toward normal.

You notice that your breathing has slowed, just as it does when you cool down from vigorous exercise.

The mind is a powerful tool. It can work for us or against us in our search for peace. We can regulate our thought process in a positive way through practice, and meditation is a part of that practice.

The Role of Medication

Your doctor may prescribe medication for any number of ailments. Most medicines are designed to treat the symptoms of disease. Some get to the heart of the problem, but most reduce the symptoms, thereby allowing the body time to heal itself. It is important for you to continue to take prescribed medicines, even if you get into a more serious meditation practice. Certainly you can discuss meditation with your doctor, and you can work with him or her to find the right dosages as your mental activity changes.

Some naturopathic medicines are designed to get the body itself to attack an illness or to overcome weakness. These tend to push the body's healing mechanisms into action. Sometimes a homeopathic remedy will evoke an emotional as well as a physiological response. We can take this as an indication that the remedy is doing its job, just as we take the reduction of symptoms as an indication that an allopathic medicine is doing its job.

Meditation can certainly reduce the need for medications. If your blood pressure and cholesterol levels are lower, you may not need all the medications you were given during an acute episode. If you no longer experience migraine headaches, naturally you can stop taking the medication for it. By the same token, you may keep a dose or two on hand for a while. Meditation is not meant to take the place of medical treatment. It is a valuable supplement to diet, exercise, and medical care.

In an interview on the Internet, Dr. Dean Ornish states:

> Meditation is great for your heart, as well as for the rest of your body. Meditation can take you to a deeper state of relaxation that is more profound even than sleep. This deep relaxation allows the heart to begin healing . . . Many studies have documented that the regular practice of meditation may lower blood pressure, reduce the frequency of irregular heart beats, and even lower cholesterol levels independent of diet. Meditation is an important part of my program for reversing heart disease.[1]

Dr. Ornish confirms here that physical healing can result from meditation, just as I mentioned earlier in this chapter that emotional healing happens. This is because you consciously are altering your perceptions, or at least your responses, to the world. You are learning how to choose your response instead of reacting.

How Much to Meditate

Previous chapters have shown that you don't need to meditate for hours at a time to achieve real benefits. Let's

---

1. Acredolo, "Q&A."

look at the evidence of the benefits. Cary Barbor has written:

> Recent research indicates that meditating brings about dramatic effects in as little as a 10-minute session. Several studies have demonstrated that subjects who meditated for a short time showed increased alpha waves (the relaxed brain waves) and decreased anxiety and depression.[2]

In chapter 1 ("Why Meditate?") I mentioned that short amounts of time are beneficial, and that you don't need to set aside hours each day. Now research documents that even ten minutes can prove very beneficial. Ten minutes a day, according to many meditation teachers, is far more beneficial than an hour and ten minutes once a week. We can set aside ten minutes a day. That is less than the average break time you get at work, for example, and a meditation break has healthy advantages.

Cary Barbor again:

> I was approached by young practitioners of transcendental meditation who asked me to monitor their blood pressure . . . what we found was astonishing. Through the simple act of changing their thought patterns, the subjects experienced decreases in their metabolism, breathing rate and brain wave frequency. These changes appeared to be the opposite of the commonly known "fight or flight" response, and I called it the "relaxation response."[3]

---

2. Barbor, "The Science of Meditation," 54.
3. Ibid., 58.

This study included a control period during which the subjects simply sat quietly, but were not meditating. The results suggest that by learning to meditate, you can effectively change your body's response to events. The "fight or flight" response triggers a surge of adrenaline, speeds the heart rate, and may prepare the blood to clot more readily. A continued, or prolonged "fight or flight" response can lead to cardiovascular stress and disease. The "relaxation response" has the reverse physical result, and is shown to reduce indicators of heart disease.

---
exercise

changing thought patterns

You have noticed by now that stray thoughts interrupt you each time you are meditating. This is inevitable. Now it is time to develop a particular line of thoughts to think about. You can consciously choose one of these when you are meditating, when you are working, or when you are feeling stress.

1. Sit and relax. Take a few deep breaths.

2. Recall a place that you enjoy visiting. Consider its colors, sounds, and smells. Notice how you relax more deeply as you think of this place. Mountain meadows are one of my favorites.

3. Put that place on your written list.

4. Recall a melody that you particularly like. It can be anything; Bach or the Beatles, even the loudest music may help you relax if it is something you really enjoy.

5. Put that melody on your list.

6. Imagine a range of colors. Choose one that feels peaceful to you, and add that to your list. I like the violet color that I see when alpha brain waves are present.

7. Remember a poem, a quotation, or words of encouragement—even the fortune you found in your last fortune cookie. Add that to the list. "Stay in the flow" works well for me.

8. Write the word "breathe" on the list too.

9. Write up your list on a small card and carry it in your wallet or purse. Put it where you keep your paper money. That way it will turn up frequently to remind you of things that are relaxing.

Whenever you read the items on your list, you will be taking a brief moment to enter a state of relaxation. As you practice, you can do this more easily. You will find that those moments are like a breath of fresh air. And speaking of breath, one or two deep breaths are enough to significantly alter your state of mind. So simple!

_____summary

We think of consciousness as being a relatively static state of mind, when in fact we enter an altered state of consciousness on a moment-to-moment basis. The flexibility of mental states is what allows us to move from one task to another very easily. Because we can change our minds so easily, meditation can help us use this capacity to make positive changes in our lives.

The next chapter considers thinking styles and how they affect meditation.

8

Thinking About Thinking

Our mind is often thinking about one thing while our body is doing another. As long as mind and body are not together, we get lost and we cannot really say that we are here.

Thich Nhat Hanh
The Heart of the Buddha's Teaching

NOW THAT YOU are meditating, at least a little bit, you may find that you are able to change your thought process so that you now think about what you think about. You analyze the sorts of thoughts that arise, and you wonder why they arise in that certain way. There may seem to be no rhyme or reason.

Most people have a preferred way to approach life. They think in certain ways and experience the world in certain ways. I want to mention two systems that consider how we think: Jungian typology and neurolinguistic programming.

Carl Jung proposed four basic personality types: thinking, feeling, sensation, and intuition. Richard Bandler and John Grinder developed an understanding of three representational systems: vision, hearing, and feeling. It is useful to note that the term "feeling" means something different in each system. Bandler and Grinder decided to use the term *kinesthetics* instead of *feeling*.

Personality Types

In the Jungian system, the four personality types represent four ways of approaching the world—four distinct ways of using the mind. Although great value is placed on thinking ability in our educational system, and intelligence is often related to this type, the other three types have equal potential. In other cultures thinking does not receive as much attention. Each of us has the capacity to use all four functions. We simply prefer one over the others, and we have a second style that we also rely on. We can develop all four, and indeed this is one of the goals of the adult developmental process.

Let us begin with sensation. Sensation is the way we perceive the raw data in the world around us. It includes sight, taste, smell, touch, and hearing. We all do this all the time. For the sensation type, the mental process is focused on sensations. Such a person learns best by doing, as learning occurs on a physical level. We know that some children can perform mathematical functions using their fingers, while others visualize a problem. The intelligence of the body is valuable to everyone.

Thinking is the function most of us think of when we consider intelligence. Jung stated that "by thinking we are able to recognize the meaning or purpose of the object we observe."[1] Just seeing something is not enough. We need to find the meaning in what we see. We analyze, catalog, and otherwise examine the incoming data. We relate it to data we have gathered previously. We move information around to see if it makes more sense to us. We may even go back to the sensations to find more information.

When Jung discusses feeling, he is referring to the process of assessing the value of the object or information we are working with. Emotions may play a part here, but Jung is referring to a primarily mental, not emotional, process. Judgment is the activity involved. How do I feel about the object? Does it please me or displease me? How much? Jung does not mean judgmental here. He is referring to evaluation that is very deeply personal.

The fourth function is intuition. This is how we relate information to time. This mental process involves what lies ahead. We might consider what can be done with an object, or how a message will fit into our future plans. We forecast the future, using intuition to speculate about information gathered through the other three functions.

---

1. Bennet, *What Jung Really Said*, 55.

identifying mental processes I

The four types of mental processes can be used to analyze your random thought process. As you meditate, consider these possibilities:

1. Are your thoughts primarily about how you perceive the immediate meditation environment? Do they focus on the cramp in your calf, the way the light from the window plays on the carpet or floor, or the creaking sounds of the building? Are you warm or cool or hungry?

2. Perhaps your thoughts are exploring the purpose of the information you are perceiving just now. You consider how the light plays on the carpet, and you consider how it is warming the fibers. You consider environmental sounds and understand that they relate to the fan switching on and off as it circulates air in the room. You notice the cramp, but relate it to your understanding of how long it takes for that muscle to tighten during meditation.

3. You may be judging your experience moment to moment. "I feel relaxed and that is a good thing." "Oops! Stray thought about my cramped leg! That's bad." "The light from the window is brighter than yesterday, and that means better weather. Good thing."

4. If you are intuitive, you are gauging the value of your meditation for the future. You are considering that

the light warming the carpet will very likely reduce your heating bill this month. You are thinking how your meditation time will prepare you for a meeting this afternoon.

The point of this exercise is to discover what your typical mental process is. Where does your mind tend to go when you give it a chance?

Many people find this mental exploration difficult or even painful. You may not want to address the way your mind works. In fact, you may expend considerable effort to avoid finding out. Remember chapter 4, "Be Kind to Yourself"? You may want to review it now. It says:

- These are your very own thoughts.

- No one is putting these thoughts into your mind.

- Your thoughts show how your mind works.

- Your thoughts reveal your mental habits.

- You can change a habit only when you understand its purpose.

Using Jungian typology, you can learn how you tend to engage in each of the mental processes. As you do this, you will undoubtedly discover both the constructive and the less constructive mental habits you possess. Then you can begin to change them.

Representational Systems

As you examine your mental process, you will find additional information. What Bandler and Grinder discovered through their research is that each of us has a typical style of accessing the information in the world. At the level of sensation in Jung's typology, we each have a dominant sense. This means that in addition to being one of the Jungian types, we also have a particular slant that we take.

The visual representational system depends on vision. How basic is that statement? What does it really mean? Visual types tend to make pictures while they are thinking. They will "see" words. They also pepper their language with visual words. In the buffet line at a restaurant, my mother would say, "What looks good to you today? Look at the wonderful red tomato."

Interestingly, I find myself more likely to respond, "I think French fries sound good." We all know that French fries don't make much sound lying there on the plate, and unless they are very crisp, they don't produce much sound in the eating process. What do I mean when I say they "sound good"? The words, spoken out loud, evoke a positive auditory response in me.

The auditory representational system depends on verbal or other sound input. An auditory type will "listen" to internal answers to questions, and then say them out loud. For example, if I am given a choice of where to go for lunch, more of my attention is on the ambient sounds of the restaurants I have visited than on the food served. Also, perhaps I like the sound of the names of foods. "Which sounds better to you: spaghetti or curried chicken?" If you think of sounds, you are auditory. If you go for the feeling in your stomach, you are the third type: kinesthetic.

The kinesthetic representational system is all about how things feel in your body. They may be associated with emotions, but the key is the associated bodily sensation. When you ask how a person feels, you may have noticed that you get different responses. Some people take some time to figure it out. You can see that they withdraw attention from the outside world to go inside. Whatever their response, if you ask where they feel it in the body, they can probably tell you. I know that worry goes to my stomach and abdomen, fear to my ribs and lungs, and love to my heart. Joy sort of bursts out at all the seams.

_____e x e r c i s e

identifying mental processes II

This exercise is very simple: Describe your experience of entering a building for the first time. Write down what you noticed.

Now look at the words you used to describe the experience. Did you mention the color of the floor, the walls, or the furniture? Did you record the music, the sound of the door closing, or the noise of feet on the tiled floor? Did you notice the feeling of comfort or tension as you entered, or perhaps the change in air temperature? We use visually vibrant words, auditorily pleasing words, and physically evocative words all the time. Each of us has a favorite among the three methods of processing information, and we reveal our preference through both verbal and body language.

Confused Yet?

Some of you are already familiar with these ways of analyzing mental processes, and you already know your favorites. Others may not see the value of considering this. Some of you have better luck asking someone else. Often it is easier to determine another person's style than it is to assess your own. The point of this is to reveal the complexity of mental process, and to suggest that you can change your thoughts by changing your perspective.

Using the two things you can discover about yourself—your Jungian personality type and the representational system you most frequently use—you can develop a set of "thoughts" that have very positive associations for you. They can become part of your list that you carry in your wallet. List peak visual experiences if you are visual, and list auditory or kinesthetic experiences if the visual representational system is not your main mode. Then when you meditate, you can label any negative thoughts as they arise, and replace them with one of your most positive associations.

enriching your experience

Relax in your normal meditative posture.

1. Take a couple of deep breaths.

2. Recall a very positive experience from the past.

3. Notice how you remember it: Do sensations, logic, feelings, or intuition dominate? Are they visual, auditory, or kinesthetic memories?

4. Now, going into the memory you have recalled, begin to extend your mind. What else comes into your awareness? Notice the additional ways there are of perceiving that positive experience.

As you practice this technique, you will discover a richness of experience that may have eluded you. This process of expanding your perceptions will carry over into daily activities. You will find yourself noticing things that you never saw, heard, or felt before. This practice can help with difficult life situations as well.

When you are in a particularly difficult situation, you may be able to "see" your way out of it by focusing on the future outcome. You may find that remembering what someone said in a previous situation is very useful now. You may even be able to close your eyes, visualize your favorite color, and relax just enough to change a less conscious reaction into a more conscious response. Recalling your meditation space can help you to relax and enter a more meditative state, no matter where you are.

By carefully considering how your mental process works, you are making friends with yourself in a new way. You acknowledge your own quirky processes, and you learn how to alter them, or at least alternate them with other, more positive images, sounds, and feelings. As you learn more about how you think, and as you broaden your possible responses, you allow for the possibility of a gap in the normal busy flow of mental information. This is where you will experience the curious, the inspirational, and the ecstatic.

In the next chapter, we explore the connection between yoga and meditation.

9

Yoga and Meditation

*True quiet means keeping still when the time has come to
keep still, and going forward when the time has come to go
forward. In this way rest and movement are in agreement
with the demands of the [moment], and thus there is light in
life.*

The I Ching, or Book of Changes

ANY ACTIVITY THAT demands close concentration has a meditative element. Yoga practices involve
three meditative components, in addition to the focus you
bring to the stretch, pose, or movement of the practice.
These are yantras, mantras, and visualizations.

During the 1960s, American culture was inundated with
elements from Hinduism that seemed quite foreign: meditation, yoga, religious practices, and attire. Actually, Christian,
Jewish, and Islamic religions include similar meditative practices. This chapter discusses yoga and its relationship to meditation, and mentions comparable elements from several

91

other religions that show the breadth of meditative practice across the world.

Yoga Practices

There are several branches of yoga, and many variations on each one of them. *Hatha yoga* is what most of us think of when yoga is mentioned. Hatha yoga incorporates breathing exercises (pranayamas), stretching and strengthening exercises (asanas), and meditation. The elegant poses of the Salute to the Sun and other hatha yoga exercises show that with practice, your body can become more flexible, even if you are rather stiff and limited in movement when you begin. Results vary, but most people gain flexibility and strength when practicing hatha yoga.

Hatha yoga also tends to improve your balance. At first you may not be able to hold a pose while standing on one foot, but as you practice, your muscles learn how to hold the posture without falling. There is a mental and emotional component of balance that develops as well. Developing balance in one area helps to improve it in all other areas.

Raja yoga does not involve difficult postures, but rather a comfortable seated posture. It concerns the freeing of yourself from limitations through right effort. It involves working directly with the mind. One sits, watches the mind, and frees the mind from distractions. One silences transient thoughts. The goal is to enter a thoughtless state in which only a unified state exists, free from duality.

Raja yoga also serves to develop four virtues. First is the friendliness you feel toward equals. Second is the compassion you feel for those less fortunate than yourself. Third is complacency, the feeling you have for superiors that is without envy. Finally, there is indifference, which is a feeling you have toward unpleasant people. These four states of mind replace such states as egoism, ignorance, attraction, aversion, and clinging. Raja yoga is directed toward changing the way thoughts arise in your mind.

Karma yoga is the yoga of work. It is concerned with finding right livelihood and then immersing yourself in it. It is finding the current and then staying in the flow. For anyone who is dissatisfied with daily life, karma yoga provides an avenue for change. You try different work until you find something that is so satisfying that you awake each day desiring to accomplish more, and you go to sleep at night satisfied that you have done well.

Bhakti yoga is the yoga of love. One who practices this yoga is cheerful and happy to be with the beloved. The strength of this yoga is that it helps one to persevere through great difficulty, as the object is love. Ultimately the focus is on the love of God, although we also love other people and things. It is my opinion that bhakti yoga leads to the marvelous experience that God loves you too. To reside in love is to be without doubt, without suffering, and without conflict.

All forms of yoga share in the elements of proper breath, proper posture, proper thought, and proper action. Each emphasizes one of these to achieve balance with the others. Each takes its own approach to meditation—on the posture, on the thought, on the work, or on love. The object of meditation in yoga may be different, but the results are strikingly similar.

Yantra

A *yantra* is a graphic representation that allows focus and concentration to deepen. One of the best-known yantras is Sri Yantra. This pattern of triangles within a frame of circles and lotus petals helps to focus the eye, and therefore the mind. Yantras are composed of geometric shapes and include no lettering or figures of deities.

The yantra is a special kind of *mandala*. At its simplest, the mandala form consists of a circle. Most mandalas define the center in some way. Some of them have complex representations of the Buddha or other religious figures. Many divide the circle to represent the four primary directions or the in-between directions.

Tibetan paintings are complex representations of the world, and at their basis is a simple mandala. These paintings (*thangkas*) are yantras of a different style. Catholic churches incorporate mandala principles in their art. Many stained glass windows are circular designs, and many crosses have a circular component to them. These are all yantras, or objects for meditation.

exercise
_____

focusing visual attention

Find a picture or an object that you particularly enjoy. It doesn't have to have a religious connotation. You can use

Figure 6. Sri Yantra.

a picture of a teacher or someone you know. However, it may be easier to choose something a bit more impersonal. I like to use natural things like flowers, or designs that are obvious mandalas (circular with defined centers).

1. Place your chosen object where you will be able to see it when you are seated.

2. Assume a comfortable seated pose.

3. Take a few deep breaths and settle into a comfortable breathing pattern.

4. Focus your eyes and your attention on the object you have selected.

5. If your attention wanders, simply come back to this focus.

6. Continue for five to ten minutes.

Notice that as you focused, your mind naturally wandered. As you came back to the object, you began to find greater detail and deeper meaning within it. You may have become curious about its nature in some way. What else did you notice about the experience?

Mantra

I often think of meditation as being a silent activity. After all, it is designed to still the mind, and stillness goes hand-in-hand with silence. Yet both Eastern and Western traditions include sound as a component of meditation. The *mantra* (similar to a prayer or spell) is a carefully designed phrase or verse that can be repeated to generate or recall a particular state of mind. Here are some examples of mantras I have found to be effective in my life.

- Hail Mary, full of Grace, the Lord is with Thee.
  Blessed art Thou among women, and Blessed is the Fruit of thy Womb, Jesus.
  Holy Mary, Mother of God,
  Pray for us sinners now and at the hour of our death.
  Amen.

- Gate, gate, paragate, parasamgate, bhodi svaha.

- Om mani padme hum.

- God and me, me and God are One.

As you can see, the language is important. By that I mean the words have to be put together in a particular way. Generally the best mantras are those that are repeated by many people many times. They connect with the Universe—the Universal Mind—in a meaningful way. They are easy to remember and they have a pleasing sound and rhythm.

exercise

reciting a mantra

Choose one of the mantras mentioned here, or choose one you have found that you like.

1. Sit in your preferred meditative posture.

2. Take one or two deep breaths.

3. Begin to recite your mantra. Continue for five to ten minutes.

Notice how your attention deepened as you repeated the words. Notice how easily you began to forget the worries of the day, no matter how serious they were. Notice how peace began to steal into your mind. What else did you notice?

Visualization

Visualization in its broadest sense includes most, if not all, our creative endeavors. We visualize a cake as we mix the individual ingredients, and we visualize an audience applauding when we construct a speech; we visualize ourselves being successful in myriad ways as we engage in daily activities.

Unfortunately, we can fall into patterns of visualizing failure as well. We sabotage our own efforts before we begin by seeing less-than-perfect outcomes. We don't trust our creative capacity, and we second-guess our decisions. Here is a meditation exercise that is designed to help stop the less constructive mental patterns.

exercise

visualizing change

1. Choose one thought or pattern of thoughts that you feel is not helpful to you. Spend a few moments thinking about it, and write down its components. Set the notes aside.

2. Seat yourself in your meditative posture.

3. Take a few deep breaths.

4. Now think about your problem thought or thought pattern. Visualize it, hear it, and feel how it feels to be in that space.

5. Now think about changing one word, one color, one sound, one thing about that thought or thought pattern. The change can be any change you choose to make.

6. Consider the thought or thought pattern again, with the one change you have made. Allow your mind to follow whatever line of thought it takes.

7. Write a few words about how you feel when you have completed the exercise.

Notice how changing one element of the pattern caused the pattern to shift. While this is not a miracle cure for negative thoughts, any change in those thoughts or thought patterns allows you to move in a more positive direction. Compare what you wrote before and after the meditation exercise. Notice any changes in how you feel.

Because you have been practicing meditation for a while, by the time you get to this page of the book, you may have developed some affinity for the state of mind you can achieve through meditation. Now you are able to introduce a problem into the setting with the expectation that you can change your perception of the problem simply by meditating. Think of it as coffee: The coffee itself is nearly black in color. Add a bit of cream, and there is a remarkable change. The black goes away, to be replaced by something different. Stir it and hear the familiar tinkle of spoon on cup. The visual image, the sound, and even the smell contribute to a certain feeling. Once you have learned to meditate, problem solving is the same.

From this chapter you can take a technique or idea that works especially well for you, and add it to your meditation practice. The variety of yogic practices tells us that no single meditation form is right for everyone. No one mantra works for all of us, and no single image will do. Meditation is a very individual practice.

The next chapter introduces some of the basic meditation practices of kundalini yoga.

10

Kundalini Meditation

*Actually Kundalini yoga means awareness. Awareness is a
finite relationship with infinity. This dormant energy is in
you. This awareness is sleeping in you and you only experience your capacity to a limit. But when it can be extended
to infinity you remain you, anyway. But in that state there
is nothing lacking.*

M.S.S. Gurucharan Singh Khalsa, compiler
Kundalini Yoga/Sadhana Guidelines

KUNDALINI ENERGY IS inherent in our bodies. In
its aroused or moving state it is frequently represented by a
feminine deity, while the dormant or static state has a
masculine representation. As you work with these two
states of energy—moving and static—you raise your
awareness through seven chakras to an eighth chakra
where, according to some kundalini teachers, you tran-
scend physical urges of all kinds and experience the
Divine.

On the physiological level, the chakras are points where nerves converge. These sites in the body are also thought to be focal points for emotional, mental, and spiritual energy. Table 1 lists the chakras with their Sanskrit names.

Kundalini yoga and meditation are designed to raise your consciousness in a very specific way. They draw your energy up the spine from the coccygeal center to the top of the spine and then to the top of the head. While spontaneous movement of kundalini energy has been known to occur, yoga and meditation provide an organized environment for its arousal. At first the flow of energy can seem powerful, foreign, and scary. Meditation and yoga give structure and discipline to an otherwise chaotic experience.

Kundalini yoga focuses meditation practice through specific breathing techniques, and through *kriyas*, or sets of exercises. The exercises often include asanas (special seated postures) and mudras (hand positions). They also include movements that are designed to stimulate specific parts of the anatomy. Mantras are chanted aloud or mentally while performing the kriyas.

The Seed Mantra in kundalini yoga is "Sat Nam." When chanting, "Sat" gets four beats and "Nam" gets one, with three rests after. "Sat" means "truth," and refers to the reality of existence. "Nam" means "name" or "identity," and refers to the vibration that creates the thing that it names. This mantra is also used in a variety of kriyas, but it is always intended to bring your mind to the realization of the Creator.

TABLE 1. Chakras

English Name	Sanskrit Name	Physical Location	Alternate System
Root Chakra	*Mooladhara*	Base of tailbone	Survival, elimination; earth element
Sacral Chakra	*Swadhisthana*	Pelvis	Sexuality and procreation; water element
Navel or Solar Plexus Chakra	*Manipura*	Navel	Power for good or evil, balance; fire element
Heart Chakra	*Anahata*	Heart, lungs	Capacity to serve, understand, and love; air element
Throat Chakra	*Vishuddhi*	Upper palate, thyroid, throat	Capacity to affect others with words; ether element
Brow Chakra	*Ajna*	Forehead	Pituitary gland (called *manas* in Sanskrit); light energy
Crown Chakra	*Sahasrara*	Top of head	Pineal gland, door of perception; element is God

_____

sat kriya

Sat Kriya is one of the simplest of the kundalini exercises. It involves one posture, one mudra, and one mantra. When you first try this exercise, you may find that you cannot continue for three minutes. Gradually you can extend the time to thirty-one minutes.

1. Sit on your heels or use a bench. Stretch your arms over your head so that your elbows are close to your ears.

2. Fold your hands together, with right thumb over the left. Unfold your index fingers and point them straight up.

3. Begin to chant "Sat Nam" ("Sat" for four beats and "Nam" for one with three beats after). On "Sat," pull the navel in toward the spine. On "Nam" relax the belly.

4. Continue for three minutes.

5. Then inhale and squeeze the back muscles tightly, from the buttocks up to the neck.

6. Mentally allow the energy to continue up to the top of the skull.

7. Relax on your back for six minutes (or twice as long as you practiced the exercise).

This exercise sounds very simple, and it does involve an easy pose. Yet it is important to try it for only three minutes when you begin, and then gradually increase to thirty-one minutes. This is because the energy movement you experience needs to be integrated in smaller steps to become part of your consciousness. Also, unless you are quite strong, your hands and arms will tire. You may also find that your feet or legs become numb when you first try this posture. The following is a statement about the results you can expect:

> In meditation you are cleansing the subconscious of fears and releasing new reservoirs of consciousness and energy to guide you. As each fear comes up and you look upon it neutrally, the fear loses its power over you. You become more flexible and feel more free.[1]

_____exercise

sat nam meditation

This is another basic kundalini practice that can fit nicely into your own personal meditation program. It, too, includes one posture, one mudra, and one mantra.

1. Sit in a relaxed cross-legged pose. If this is uncomfortable at first, you can support your knees with small pillows to take the strain off the joints. Be careful to keep the spine straight as you do this exercise.

---

1. Singh Khalsa, *Kundalini Yoga/Sadhana Guidelines*, 15.

2. Put the palms of your hands together, and with the thumbs touch your sternum. The hands are very close to the chest.

3. Close your eyes and focus on a point on your brow just above and between the eyes. If you do this properly, you will find it is nearly impossible to think a negative thought.

4. Inhale deeply and concentrate on the breath.

5. As you exhale, say the Seed Mantra. The word "Sat" gets a count of seven, and the word "Nam" gets a count of one. On each count of "Sat," feel energy rising within you, beginning at the base of the spine and radiating upward through the body. (See Table 1 for information about the seven centers.)

6. Continue for fifteen minutes. This exercise can be increased to thirty-one and a half minutes or more each day.

This meditation is thought to change habitual thought patterns. It is largely the mantra that accomplishes the change, but the breath and posture enable you to feel energy movement in your body as well as in the mind. This meditation opens the mind to new experiences, and is a good one for beginning other meditations.

Kundalini yoga as taught by Yogi Bhajan is a rigorous exercise program as well as a meditation system. Many of the poses and movements will challenge you, even if you are quite strong. The two exercises included here are basic ones, and even they may take some time for you to sustain them for the suggested period of time.

What I have found with most movement meditations is that you have to first concentrate on the movement to be sure you are doing it properly. The same holds for whatever breathing process is involved. The postures, movements, breaths, and mantras are not accidental. They are put together to accomplish very specific purposes. As you develop skill in the exercise, you will find that your mind gets into the rhythm too. You'll find that you are less distracted, and that calmness enters into the process, even when you are doing more strenuous kriyas.

If you would like more information about kundalini, Ravindra Kumar's *Kundalini for Beginners* provides an authoritative look at the philosophy of this system, which is sometimes called "the shortest path to God."

The next two exercises are described as part of longer kriyas, but they can be used independently with good effect, or as part of your meditation each day. Both take only a few minutes, but are not suited for public situations.

exercise

meditation for digestion and to strengthen your aura

This meditation, if practiced regularly, helps to resolve digestive problems. It also strengthens the arms and remagnetizes the aura. In the short term you may find that you get a "buzz" from this one that is quite pleasant. It is important to rest a few minutes afterward.

1. Sit in a comfortable cross-legged meditation pose. If you sit in a chair instead, make sure the back of the chair will not interfere with the movement of your arms. You may want to use a bench or stool instead of a chair for this meditation.

2. Begin by stretching your arms straight out in front of you with your palms about six inches apart and facing each other.

3. Inhale and bring the arms to the side and back, stretching them toward each other in back of you. The thumbs continue to point upward.

4. Exhale and bring your arms back to the first position straight in front of you.

5. Continue for three minutes. The breathing is deep and strong and not too fast. It feels like a pumping motion.

6. Rest for several minutes by either sitting or lying on your back.

This is a vigorous exercise. The first time you try it, you may find that three minutes is too long. You can build up to the three minutes if necessary. You will feel energized when you are finished. Sometimes people will also feel lightheaded afterward, which is why the rest period is essential.

laughing meditation

For a different kind of lightness, this simple meditation works really well. This meditation is sometimes the last step in a kriya of several positions, and can be used to conclude your meditation sessions.

1. Lie on your back with your hands at your sides.

2. Open your mouth and begin to laugh loudly. Use your diaphragm to push the laugh out. Continue for one minute.

3. Relax for one minute.

4. Repeat.

5. Relax for a few minutes.

This exercise helps to circulate energy throughout the body. It will cheer you up too!

Kundalini yoga, when practiced regularly, enhances physical strength, flexibility, and mental relaxation. By concentrating on the movements and on the mantras, you reduce the extraneous "chatter" and focus instead on patterns that are proven to elevate your consciousness to a new level of awareness.

The next two chapters go beyond the movement involved in yoga exercises to consider walking, running, and athletic performance. These will demonstrate that meditation is not limited to sitting on a cushion, but can be carried with you out into the world.

11

Walking Meditation

In general, a leftward movement indicates movement towards the unconscious, while a rightward (clockwise) movement goes towards consciousness.

Carl G. Jung
Mandala Symbolism

MANY CULTURES INCLUDE walking meditation as part of their spiritual practices. Sometimes the walking is oriented to a physical destination, as in the vision quest of North American Indians or the walkabout of Australian Aborigines. In both cases, walking takes the individual to another place—both physically and spiritually. Another example is the labyrinth, where one walks around and around to slowly approach a central point.

In other cases walking really doesn't take you to a distant location, or certainly not to a particular location. One example is the square or circular covered walkways that surround the well in monasteries, where monks walk around and around the central space. In this case the path itself is well-known, yet there is no destination.

Walking around the inner courtyard of a monastery provides a defined environment for walking meditation. The familiarity of the space allows you to go deep within yourself without fear of encountering obstacles or losing your balance. Your eyes are open to see what is ahead of you, but your attention can have a primary focus elsewhere. You can immerse yourself in the peace that is associated with the space.

A second example of a walking meditation without a destination is aimless wandering—walking without a planned destination while maintaining awareness of one's surroundings. In this case neither the path nor the destination is fixed.

_____e x e r c i s e

walking meditation I

Find a place, either indoors or outside, where you can walk in a circle. Walk along the same line each time you go around as you do this exercise.

1. Begin walking counterclockwise at a comfortable pace. Breathe naturally. This is the direction of many racetracks. Walk for about five minutes, focusing your eyes on the path, but allowing yourself to become aware of the things in your immediate environment.

2. Rest for a moment outside the circle you have been walking.

3. Now walk the same path in a clockwise direction for about five minutes.

4. What do you notice about the different directions? Do you feel and think differently? Which way is more comfortable? Which way is more challenging?

5. You may want to try this exercise at different times of the day when the light comes from different directions.

Walking meditation helps to clear your mind of its usual chatter in a different way from more static practices. The idea is that you bring your full awareness to whatever you perceive as you are walking. As you get into this style, you find that you see all sorts of interesting things in the environment that you may have formerly missed. The beauty of tiny flowers, the sounds of the environment, and the manifold differences in the leaves of grass, plants, and trees all become more apparent. Often you feel more connected to the physical world through this kind of attention. You may even begin to have compassionate feelings toward your surroundings.

When I am in this meditative space, I am moved to pick up bits of trash that detract from the beauty of or even harm the environment. Think of the signs posted by the highway that say the next three miles are cared for by a particular group or business. The individuals who go out to this piece of road have to bring their full awareness to the clean-up effort. In the process they doubtlessly discover all sorts of things about roadside flora and fauna that they didn't know. When you are looking closely for what does not belong, you cannot help noticing what does belong.

walking meditation II

This exercise is best done on a day that is neither too warm nor too cool. Morning or evening is best. You may want to shade your eyes if the sun is bright.

1. Find a place that is familiar to you, but one you don't often visit. It can be a park, a trail, or a neighborhood near you.

2. Begin your walk of ten or fifteen minutes with nothing in mind as a path or destination. You have no goals concerning distance or direction. Walk at a leisurely pace. You should be able to have a conversation easily, although you will be alone, so that is not likely.

3. Observe the sights and sounds around you. Notice the plants or animals along the path.

4. Stop to enjoy your environment as you move along.

Labyrinths

Walking a labyrinth is another sort of experience altogether. You are following a prescribed path that winds and folds back on itself in multiple ways—the folds are determined by the design. You circle, approach, and retreat from the center several times before you reach the goal. You follow both clockwise and counterclockwise paths, with left and right turnings. The labyrinth meditation is designed to bring you into direct contact with your own thoughts and feelings.

Many people do not find the labyrinth meditation calming, especially not at first. There can be significant frustration involved in this path. The design is on the floor or ground. You can see the center, yet you are turned away again and again. This is rather like the psychological path toward wholeness: You feel yourself almost there, only to be turned away to consider yet another flaw or fallacy in your thinking. When you find yourself at the actual center of the labyrinth, it may even come as something of a surprise.

With a labyrinth, the path remains the same. You will always need to take the single available left- or right-hand turn to arrive at the center. As you turn your attention to the path of the moment, the process causes you to shed the problems of the day. This meditation brings you fully into the present. Even after you have walked the same pattern many times, it is always possible to discover something new—about the path or about yourself.

On the psychological level, you may never find the precise, true center of your being. You gain familiarity with its

Figure 7. Labyrinth.

environment, certainly, and you learn how to remain closer to the center. You resolve the psychic distractions so that you can approach the center more easily over time.

The meditation labyrinth is different from a maze. As I have mentioned, the labyrinth has one path to the center that traverses all four quarters of a circle or square. A maze, on the other hand, has blind paths, and may have intersections as well. There may be several solutions to a maze, while the meditation labyrinth has only one. A maze can become a labyrinth, however, if you follow a

Figure 8. Maze.

definite path through it, such as always taking the right-hand turns.

Walking meditation has advantages and disadvantages. Weather is a significant factor if you walk outdoors. Concentration may be difficult if you are too warm, too cold, or too wet, for example. One advantage, however, is that you don't become uncomfortable in a particular sitting posture. Another advantage is that walking is a

117

weight-bearing exercise, so you become more physically fit while you meditate. Of course, sitting meditation has health advantages as well. (See chapter 15, "Healing Meditation," for more information on the health benefits of meditation.)

The next chapter is about jogging, running, and other kinds of athletic performance. We will explore how meditation can benefit physical performance, and we will consider how the performance itself can become a meditative process.

12

Athletic and Other Kinds of Performance

A large part of my attraction to running was its meditative qualities—the calming process of quiet, deep-thought, long-distance running allows for. I enjoyed not only a physical "high" from the exercise, but an emotional release as well.

Jacine Harrington
The Beauty of Yoga

MANY ATHLETES HAVE talked about the "high" they get from their best performances. We can see the ecstatic looks on their faces that go far beyond the joy of competing and winning. We see the euphoria in the midst of the pain of strength and endurance tests. We know it is more than a mental satisfaction. It reaches to emotional and even spiritual levels.

There are examples of athletes who are so naturally skilled that they seem born to do whatever sport they attempt; they learn almost instantly and they have careers filled with highlights. We enjoy the singing abilities of individuals who began when they were very young and continue well past middle age. We are astonished by the insights of scientists or mathematicians, and we wonder how they ever thought up some of those theories that then change our lives forever. Much of this natural success can be attributed to some form of meditation.

The amazing athlete Jim Thorpe provides an example of meditation's role in natural success. Thorpe was born in 1887. He attended an American Indian school beginning in 1904. He played football, but he became a star on the track. One day while he was cleaning up around the track, he asked to try the high jump. The bar was then at 5'9". Even without a warm-up he easily cleared the bar.

Thorpe was a natural runner too. He was able to win both the pentathlon and decathlon in the 1912 Olympic games. Before that he had pitched baseball for two years and played more football. Not many individuals excel at over a dozen sports. So how did he do it, aside from having tremendous natural talent?

Athletic lore has it that Thorpe only had to watch someone performing in order to learn how to do each event. He had an intense personal desire to test himself against other athletes, and he consistently prevailed. His method almost surely had something of meditation to it. He was able to observe an athletic event, think about how it was done, and then do it better than the trained competitor. This ability is called *bare attention*. He was able to eliminate all distractions in the environment and in his mind, focus on the precise physical effort involved, and then duplicate that effort.

Mozart engaged in bare attention as well. He was able to listen to a piece of music once, and then write the notation. He was also able to listen, and then immediately play the music and embellish what he had heard.

Some people have the capacity to remember word for word what they have read. Others hear a song and can then sing it without error. Many of us have at least one interest that so captures our attention that we don't hear what is happening around us. We observe this kind of rapt attention in children at play.

Through meditation we can develop the capacity for bare attention. By focusing on the breath or a meditation object, by chanting mantras, and by practicing, we cultivate this ability. Through regular meditation practice, we learn to slip into this mental frame more and more easily. Even in stressful times we are able to let go of the distractions while we sit, totally focused seemingly on nothing.

To enhance performance, we carry the relaxed mental state into the performance. We are not easy to distract from the task. In watching Marion Jones prepare for a race, you observe her going through precisely the same motions. You might only notice this if the race is restarted. She walks back and forth as she mentally prepares for the race. She removes her warm-up clothing. She pounds her leg muscles, and she twists her body just so. She sets herself in the blocks exactly the same way each time. As she focuses, she looks down the track to the tape and slowly lowers her head. For all it seems, these starts could be instant replays. This mental and physical preparation is a form of meditation.

Such preparation can be done with the mind with no physical activity attached. Thinking through an upcoming challenge provides significant preparation for any kind of performance. Thinking with the single-mindedness of Jim Thorpe or Marion Jones adds a dimension to an already skilled performance level. Whatever the activity you engage in—work, play, or relaxation—a more complete focus leads to better experience. Some people say they lose themselves in the moment. This is a sign that they have moved the ego out of the way and allowed a single focus to dominate.

---
exercise

practicing to improve skills

Before you begin your meditation, think about the activity you are working on. Think about how you have practiced, and think about what your teacher or coach has told you.

1. Seat yourself comfortably.

2. Begin slow, deep breathing.

3. Visualize your activity as though it is being performed perfectly by someone else. Notice the details of the performance. Try to identify the balance in that person's body and/or mind.

4. Now visualize the performance as though you are the performer. See the performance from your perspective. If you are playing the piano, visualize your hands on the keys. If you are on the athletic field, visualize the scene as though you are there. Visualize how you get to the piano or the starting line or whatever, as well as the performance itself.

5. Experience the feel of your body as you go through the performance. Notice how it feels to be perfectly balanced throughout the activity in both body and mind. Notice the emotional quality of your performance.

6. If you experience a break in concentration, you may want to rerun that part of the performance. Can you tell what happens to break your concentration?

7. Now run through your performance, imagining that you are doing it perfectly. Imagine that you are acting from a calm center, exerting just the right amount of physical, mental, emotional, and even spiritual energy to achieve a perfect performance.

8. Now visualize how you respond to your own perfect performance.

9. Complete your meditation.

This exercise may take considerable effort to achieve perfection. Just as you have performance limitations, the meditation itself may be filled with distractions. The better the focus you can achieve in your meditation, the better the performance you can give.

The steps here have been kept very simple. You may want to incorporate other steps if your performance is complex. Remember to visualize the performance from both points of view—watch someone else perform perfectly, and then see yourself as the performer, seeing it through your own eyes, hearing with your own ears, and so on. There is a reason for this. We learn by watching others perform, or by listening to their performance. We also learn through our own practice. When the moment comes for your perfect performance, you will have integrated what you have seen with what you are doing, and the performance's point of balance will be inside your own body where it belongs.

Performance as Meditation

Now let's turn the tables and view performance itself as a meditation. As a performance nears perfection, it becomes an ecstatic experience. You put everything you have—body, mind, and spirit—into the performance, and it takes you to the level of a peak experience.

In order to bring your whole self to the performance, you must enter a space in which nothing else exists. It is not that other things don't matter, they simply don't exist in that moment. In your meditation practice, you have had glimpses of space—of the nothingness of the void. You have found that those moments come unannounced. You generally cannot summon them on demand, yet they come. Through practice, you create a moment in time and place where you can produce your best, strongest, and most perfect performance.

There is great calm in the midst of your expenditure of effort. Instead of your performance being a thing you do outside your normal routine—an event—it is all of you in that moment, and you are all of it. By developing a profound focus, you are able to eliminate all distractions for the duration of the performance. The reason for striving to get there no longer matters. The audience is no longer important. There is only you performing. Even your competitors dim in that moment. When you are finished, you know you have given the best you have in you.

_____exercise

giving your best

1. Do it. All the time, every day, moment to moment.

_____summary

Actually, I believe we all do the best we can all the time. After all, why would we do otherwise? Would we think up the very best choice, and then do something else? Probably not. Meditation is a practice that helps us to identify even better choices in our lives. Meditation helps to clear out repetitive—but not always helpful—mental behaviors. These are replaced with physical relaxation, mental clarity, and emotional calm, in which good decisions may arise.

The next chapter is about dreams, a source of information from within the self and an appropriate subject for meditation.

13

Dream Meditations

Everyone dreams every night. Dreaming is an activity that is almost as familiar as eating or walking, yet our dreams often mystify us. . . . [Your] dream is yours and no one else's. And therefore it is your dream to interpret.

Stephanie Clement
Dreams: Working Interactive

MEDITATION CAN BE a wonderful adjunct to dream work. The world of dreams is rich with information for you about your own life, about the people around you, and about your connection to the Universe. In exploring your dreams you are connecting directly to the inner spirit—one of the goals of meditation. You can connect your dream world to your conscious world through specific meditation practices.

The following are three meditation paths that can lead to greater dream understanding:

1. You can use meditation to go back into your dream to complete an action or to gain understanding.

2. You can re-enter the dream and become one dream character or image. The resulting experience can reveal important connections to your waking life.

3. If there is a specific message that came to you in a dream—something that was said that resonates with your conscious mind—you can use that statement as a mantra in your meditation.

To work with your dreams, it is helpful to record them. The following are some thoughts about how to record your dreams from my book *Dreams: Working Interactive:*

- Keep paper and a pen near your bed so you don't have to look for them.

- Record the dream exactly as it occurred to the extent that this is possible. Because dream details fade over the minutes or hours after awakening, it is essential to record the dream immediately.

- Record the dream without any editorial comments. Become a trained observer of your own dreams. Don't analyze them as you write, or edit out inconvenient content. By the same token, don't obsess about every tiny detail of pattern and color. Simply record the places, characters, and events.

- Allow the spirit of the dream to imbue your words when it will.

• Tell all dreams as though they are happening in the present, as this makes it easier to re-enter the dream and recall it more completely.

After you have recorded the dream, you can go back and fill in any additional details you recall. The first draft of your dream may look like one of the papers you wrote in school, with little balloons of added information, crossed-out words, and irregular handwriting.

_____exercise

going back into the dream

There are a number of ways to re-enter a dream. The following is a way to do this through your meditation using a written record of your dream.

1. As you prepare to meditate, reread the dream. Find something in the dream that attracts your attention. It can be a dream character, a color, a place, an animal, a symbol, or the action of the dream. It can be the one thing that makes the most sense, or it can be the one thing that seems out of place in the dream.

2. Begin your meditation. Breathe slowly and fully. Relax the tension in your body.

3. As you breathe more deeply, recall the dream element. Focus on it. Notice how it feels to you.

4. Allow your mind to approach the dream element. Follow your random thoughts about it. Let yourself move from observer to participant as you re-enter the dream.

5. Because you are awake, you can move around in the dream. You can take actions that you may not have been capable of while you were dreaming:

   a. You can complete the dream if it was interrupted. Once you re-enter the dream, allow the action to unfold. Think about what you want to happen.

   b. You can leave the dream. If the dream is uncomfortable in any way, you can leave the dream, sit calmly for a few minutes, and either try again or simply complete your meditation.

   c. You can recall greater detail. You are back in the dream, so you can look around you, you can hear, and you can even smell the smells of the dream.

6. When you are satisfied, when the dream stops its action, or when you have used up the time you have available, you can withdraw from the dream. As you do this, express your respect for whatever has occurred.

7. Write down the new information from the dream, any insights that you have gained, or feelings that are significant.

8. Conclude your meditation. Allow a few minutes to re-orient yourself to your waking world.

What new information have you gained, either about the dream itself or about your dreaming process? Does your meditation help with dream recall? Remember what worked for the next time you want to explore a dream. Remember, too, that working with dreams is a sort of ritual process, and is worthy of the respect you bring to it.

exercise

focusing on a specific dream image or person

In the previous exercise, you used one element of your dream as an entry point. Now you will focus on one element of the dream and explore it. This time the dream action will not move. Instead, you will be analyzing the character, image, or symbol in detail.

1. Reread the dream to recall what you already know about the image you will explore.

2. Begin your meditation as usual. Breathe slowly and deeply.

3. As you relax, focus your mind on the image you wish to explore.

4. Examine every detail you can perceive. Remember, you may be able to hear the character, and that will help you to explore visual details. You may see the image more clearly, and that will help you to engage your other senses.

5. As you explore your perceptions, let yourself approach and withdraw from the image. Change your point of view. Does the image have a back side or a side view?

6. Approach the image and let yourself touch it, or merge with it. Notice what you see, feel, or otherwise experience.

7. Notice how the image changes as you examine it.

8. Notice how your feelings and thoughts change as you examine it.

9. When you are satisfied, withdraw from the image and from the dream.

10. Record your observations.

11. Complete your meditation.

Often we struggle with difficult dreams. We try to apply conscious logic to understand their messages. The dream has a logic of its own that is amenable to examination. By re-entering the dream to interact with a dream figure, you can use your meditative skills to access that internal logic and explore it more fully. In doing this you establish a closer connection between your waking consciousness and your dream mind. Even the scariest dreams can offer useful information when approached in this way.

recalling a dream message and repeating it like a mantra

Some dreams have an impressive character—even an archangel—that pronounces a truth. The words are imprinted on your mind, even though you may entirely forget how you came to be in the presence of the dream messenger. When you awaken, you find that you write the message down and it may be the only thing you recall.

Sometimes the dream message is embedded in a dream drama. All the characters' actions seem to point to this one line from the play, and the line may not fit the rest of the play at all. On the other hand, it may seem totally ordinary. The unordinary thing is that you remember the words so clearly. Often the message is short and snappy, like an advertising jingle. Even if the words don't seem all that significant, it may be useful to work with them in your meditation.

1. Reread the dream to recall the words.

2. Begin your meditation.

3. As you relax and slow the breath, begin to repeat the words. I find it is helpful to say them out loud, not just run through them mentally.

4. You may find that the words flow slowly and rhythmically, or you may find they burst out fast and loud.

5. Whatever the words sound like, continue repeating them. Remember to breathe as you repeat them.

6. Continue for several minutes.

7. Conclude your meditation.

What did you notice about the words? How did it feel to say them out loud over and over? Did the rhythm or meaning of them change? Did the words themselves change? How do you feel now after using the words as a mantra in your meditation?

Because working with dreams is an interactive process between your conscious mind and your subconscious mind, you will find that follow-up dreams are connected to the ones you work with in meditation. A dream character may change his or her appearance, dress, or mannerisms. A symbol may develop and grow in unexpected directions. The action of the dream may play out differently in a later dream.

By recording dreams and working with them in your meditation, you enrich the conversation between your conscious mind and your dream mind. One outcome is deepening the connection between the two. Another significant outcome is the alignment of your waking activities with your inner spirit. As the two become more aligned, you achieve a sense of deeper purpose and security. You know you are on the right track more often, and you feel the energies around you more fully. This kind of insight allows you to manage difficulties with greater calm and presence of mind. It also allows you to enter into the joys of life more easily and completely.

Using Meditation to Call a Dream

Once you have established a flexible connection with your dream mind, you can begin to use dreams as a regular part of your problem-solving strategy. Calling a dream may involve asking a very specific question, or it can be more general. For example, if you are seeking a new job or career, you might ask for a dream to clarify what is the best work environment, or the best place to which to relocate, or the best kind of people with whom to work. General questions generate very evocative dreams. You may have a precise question like, "Which car should I purchase?" Your dream mind can reveal subtle considerations that influence your decision.

---
exercise

calling a dream

1. Think about your question. Write it down.

2. When you are ready to go to sleep, meditate for a few minutes.

3. Begin your meditation as you normally do.

4. As you relax, hold the question in your mind. Visualize the words. Repeat the question aloud several times.

5. Complete your meditation as usual.

As you go to sleep, recall your question once more, and then let it go. Affirm that you will recall your dreams when you awake.

You will dream, and the dreams you have will relate to your question. The exact relationship may not be obvious at first though. You can use the exercises in this chapter to re-enter the dreams you recall in order to clarify the answer. You may have to try for several nights in order to gain clarity. As you practice this technique, you will find that the answers come through much more easily, and you enrich your waking life with the symbols, characters, and events of your dreams.

<hr>

summary

Because meditation addresses the nature of your whole consciousness, it is a wonderful tool to aid in understanding dreams. Any message that emerges from the less conscious level of the mind can be understood more clearly when your mind is calm, and meditation provides a degree of calmness. In addition, you learn to access intuition concerning dreams more directly through meditation.

The next chapter introduces Tarot and other symbols as objects of focus in your meditations.

14

Tarot and Other Archetypal Meditations

> *The Tarot images are symbols that speak directly to your personal unconscious, because symbolism is the language of the unconscious.*
>
> Janina Renée
> *Tarot for a New Generation*

THE TAROT PROVIDES a systematic set of archetypal expressions that can be very useful in meditation. If you are familiar with Tarot, you probably have a favorite deck that you can use in meditation. If you have not tried Tarot, now may be a good time to get a deck and begin your exploration of a wonderful set of images that reflect human wisdom and experience. This chapter explores ways to use the Tarot in meditation, and suggests a way to explore any archetype you wish. It also includes suggestions for using meditation as an aid in studying the Tarot or any symbol system.

meditation on one card

1. Select a particular card from the Tarot deck or shuffle and draw one at random to set the tone for the day.

2. Place the card where you can look at it easily. You may want to stand it up against something else. Make sure there is no reflection to interfere with seeing it clearly.

3. Begin your meditation as usual.

4. As you relax your breathing, focus your attention on the card you have selected.

5. Explore the images and colors in the card.

6. Allow yourself to enter the world of the card as you have done in dream meditations.

7. Do this for several minutes.

8. Complete your meditation.

Notice what feeling you get from this card today. The cards can evoke different thoughts and feelings at different times, so it is important not to hold on too tightly to specific ideas about a card. For example, if you have chosen the Emperor for your meditation, at one time you may identify with the solidity of the card—it is an expression of manifestation in the physical world. At another time you may find that the Emperor seems to speak to you as a powerful ally. At still another time he may seem very busy holding his tools of office—too busy to actually accomplish anything else.

As you meditate, allow the card and its images to join with your considerations for the day. The card will seem different based on what is in your mind. If you have a busy schedule of activities, the card may reflect that, or it may reflect a calm demeanor that you can take along with you. If you have an open day with no special plans, the card may suggest an activity for you. The card may make you aware of something that you had previously missed. It could be a signal or a warning, or just a tone that sets up the rest of the day.

exercise

meditation to answer a question

If you have a specific question or problem, you can combine meditation with Tarot to help find the answer.

1. Think about your question for a moment, shuffle, and then draw a random card from the deck.

2. Like step 2 in the previous meditation, place the card where you can see it.

3. Begin to meditate, immersing yourself in the colors and images of the card.

4. Continue meditating for a comfortable length of time.

5. Complete your meditation.

This process will help you combine your question with the Tarot image you have drawn at random from the deck. Even if the card seems at first to have nothing to do with your question, do the meditation anyway. There are a few possible outcomes:

- The card redirects you to a more compelling question that you have overlooked.

- The card provides you with an unexpected answer.

- The synthesis of card and question results in a potential solution.

- At the very least, your natural curiosity is directed toward problem-solving and away from worry.

_____exercise

pursuing a meditation image

When a certain image arises in meditation again and again, it is powerful and significant. Sometimes we cannot determine what the significance is without some help. If you have such an image floating around from time to time, the Tarot can help you see its significance.

1. Think about the image you want to understand. Notice its shape and color(s).

2. Begin your meditation with a few relaxing moments of steady breathing.

3. Now go through your Tarot deck until you come to a card that strongly resembles your meditation image. It can be the same figure, similar symbols, or just similar colors. What is important is that the card has a similar feeling tone to the meditation image.

4. You can now go one of two directions: (a) Use the card as a meditation focus and continue your process, or (b) examine the card analytically. Consider each symbol in the card and recall what you know about the symbol. You may recall other times this card has come up in readings. Do some research on the card or its symbols.

This exercise provides two different mental avenues to learn about an image that has come up repeatedly for you. Both can reveal additional data for your consideration. You may want to combine the methods to get the most information possible. Later you may find that the meditation image has changed. It may not arise again, or it may show you in some way that your efforts have had an impact. In paying attention in this way, you honor your internal process by spending time to understand it.

Studying Tarot Using Meditation

As you study Tarot or any symbolic system, meditation helps you integrate your studies. Often we focus on a subject in a very conscious way and then have to wait for intuition to kick in. Meditation provides a more direct way to access the less conscious side of the intuitive mind.

If you have studied Tarot, you probably have one or more decks of cards and books and other information about what the cards mean. These tools present the human figures, colors, and symbols for each card, and discuss their meanings. As you use the cards, you commit this information to memory. The exercises in this chapter provide several ways to use the individual cards to access intuitive information through meditation to supplement your studies.

To study Tarot systematically, you can focus on the cards in an orderly way instead of drawing a card at random. You may wish to meditate on the major arcana's progression of symbols and archetypal energies. If you do meditate on them in order, you place yourself within that order and you experience the depth and richness of the images in a new, progressive way.

Another approach is to meditate on card number one in the major arcana, along with the Aces from each of the suits as well. These five cards form a set of symbols. The Magician presents the overarching archetypal expression of directed energy, and the Aces reveal how this archetype expresses itself through each of the four elements. By using the major arcana with the suit cards, you may deepen your understanding of the first ten cards of the major arcana.

You can then make notes on what you have learned through your meditation on the cards, facts you have learned from books, and readings you have done for yourself or others. Then when these cards appear in future readings, you can refer back to your notes. If you don't want to refer to your notes, you can also focus on the card in a meditative way and gather meaning from the context of the reading.

Other Meditations on Archetypes

These meditation methods can be used to explore any person, image, or feeling that dominates your meditation practice. However, you don't need Tarot cards to explore an image. You can find a picture in a book or use a piece of music as background sound while you meditate. You can surround yourself with objects of a certain color that speak to the symbol or archetype you are exploring.

Be creative in your explorations. Meditation can be very helpful in resolving conflicts when you explore the elements of the problem in the ways suggested here. It is often true that the act of paying attention is all that is needed to provide helpful answers. The use of Tarot cards or some other specific tool only serve to enhance your insight because of the meaningful organization of symbols in the image. With these tools, you focus your meditation to include perceptions directly associated with the problem.

As you try these exercises, you may want to keep some notes about your experiences. Certain images have a habit of turning up again during meditation, in dreams, or out there in the world. Some of our most interesting experiences involve these seemingly coincidental repetitions. Recognizing connections makes sense of life and enriches your experience of it. Images and colors can enhance your capacity for healing.

The next chapter explores methods of healing using meditation.

15

Healing Meditation

Healing is not creating a perfect idea or a perfect body; it is revealing an idea which is already perfect.

Ernest Holmes
The Science of Mind

USING MEDITATION FOR healing can be personally beneficial, and it can act as a supplement or vehicle for healing others. First I want to focus on self-healing. If you are tired, have a headache or sore muscles, or are emotionally distraught, you can heal yourself by focusing and redirecting your attention. When I was in a car accident, I had major pain due to a broken jaw and other injuries. I tried to escape the pain, but found that I was unable to do so. The following exercise is one I found helped me to control the pain, even to the point where I was free from it. You may think this meditation is silly, but I assure you that it works quite well if you can overcome your self-consciousness and play with it.

exercise for self-healing

1. Sit, recline, or lie in a comfortable position. Be sure your hands and arms are resting without tension.

2. Take several deep breaths, and rest your eyes. I found that closing my eyes was very helpful, as it is easier to visualize that way.

3. Think of your body as a factory filled with hundreds or even thousands of workers, each performing their tasks in shifts. Feel energy moving in your body. At first the pain is about all you will feel, but continue to breathe slowly, and you will find you become aware of other parts of your body.

4. Visualize the "workers" in your "factory." You may be pleasantly surprised to find that they take on fun or unusual characteristics. They may have uniforms, for example, or they may look like blood corpuscles moving or dancing around the system. Just see them for what they are to you.

5. Knowing that it is about time for a shift change, thank your workers for doing their jobs. Then ask them to do one more thing before they go off their shift: Ask them to take their "tools" with them to the place where you are experiencing the pain. Ask

them to clean up that area so that you will not have that pain.

6. Now simply observe what they do while maintaining your breathing in a relaxed state.

7. When they are done, thank them again.

In my meditation, my factory workers bring ordinary household brooms with them, and they sweep away the debris at the site of my pain. By doing this they allow the healthy tissue to regenerate and to occupy its proper space. In your meditation they can bring slide rules to measure it, or whatever tools they choose. I have found that my "workers" are also able to dissolve tension, clear away the results of a virus, and assist digestion. They are naturally skilled in maintaining my body—after all, they live in it— and it doesn't matter how I visualize them. What matters is the mental intention to effect healthy change.

You may modify this meditation to suit yourself. Every-one has their own triggers and sensitive points, so your "fac-tory" will look different from mine. This kind of healing improves with practice. At first you may not even detect a noticeable change. However, over a period of days you will notice significant improvement in both your ability to maintain the visualization, and the positive effects it has.

Healing Others

There are numerous spiritual methods for focusing and directing healing energy toward others, but I will not explore them in great depth. Reiki, Healing Touch, and Polarity Therapy are examples of systems that train the focus and direction of your energy to help others. Buddhism has a practice of taking the pain of others and sending healing and love back in its place. Aikido is associated with ki healing. (*Ki*, or *ch'i*, is energy that flows naturally through the healthy body.) Acupressure and acupuncture allow one person to help redirect energy in another person's body.

I want to present a way to help others without touching them, and indeed without even being close to them in terms of space. Before you ever get into the position of needing to help, you will want to develop a sense of yourself, and your place in the world. One way to do this is through ki meditation.

exercise
_____

ki meditation

I learned this meditation as part of Aikido training. The method begins with sitting in a kneeling position. This is hard to do at first, but after a period of time you will find that the posture is not painful. You can place a round cushion under you to relieve stress on the knees. You may find that your feet and legs go to sleep, so be careful when you get up and take your first few steps.

1. Wear loose comfortable clothing. In class we wore uniforms with loose pants suitable for martial arts.

2. Kneel and arrange your feet and legs. I found this posture easier with my knees several inches apart and my toes close together. If you use a cushion, your feet will be apart. If the posture is not possible, sit in a chair with your feet flat on the floor.

3. Place your hands on your thighs in a comfortable position. Your back should be straight and your head held up.

4. Gaze at a spot on the floor about six feet in front of you.

5. Begin slowly breathing in and out. As you breathe in and out, think of yourself going deep within yourself. With each breath, feel yourself going deeper and deeper. Become aware of sensations—sounds, tastes, smells—whatever you experience about yourself.

6. After a few minutes, think of going out from yourself. Become aware of other people in the room, sounds in the building, sounds you can hear outside the building. Continue to expand your awareness, enlarging your sphere of attention.

7. After a few minutes, reverse and return into yourself. Continue the meditation by reversing directions every few minutes.

You will soon discover that you can become very self-involved when you go within. Even more surprising, you will discover that you can expand your attention to include the stars and galaxies. At first you may feel yourself jerk in and out of awareness. With practice you will be able to follow your breathing and experience a profound relationship to your inner being and to the Universe.

Ki meditation helps you to become more aware of your surroundings and of yourself. It is very useful in martial arts training, as it helps you to focus your mind on the tasks of the training, your relationship to your partner/opponent, and the flow of energy between you.

It is this awareness that is engaged when you are helping others—you are definitely yourself, and you are part of a broader Universe that is just as real. Kiatsu is a method of healing touch associated with Aikido. The basic concept of it is to focus your energy, and, while maintaining balance yourself, direct your energy into the other person through your hands or thumbs. Your energy is used to help move energy in the other person's body. If you are interested in learning such hands-on healing techniques, you will find resources in the bibliography of this book.

exercise

taking and sending meditation

While the foundation of meditation is a bit scary to the beginner, the fact is that it is easy to do, and actually helps everyone involved. Compassion makes us want to help others, and when we do something for them, we also feel better about ourselves. The goal of this meditation is to take on the suffering of another, and to return healing and love. For example, if someone is afraid, you recognize his or her fear and take it on as your own, then send back love and feelings of confidence. You do this consciously and willingly.

1. Settle yourself in a comfortable posture.

2. Begin breathing slowly and evenly.

3. As you breathe in, imagine yourself taking on the fear or pain of the other person.

4. As you breathe out, imagine yourself sending out love and healing.

5. Continue the practice for several minutes.

Notice that at first you may feel agitated, but that as you continue, you experience greater calm and peace. This meditation is an act of compassion for others, and it also is an act of understanding yourself. You recognize your own sensitivity to emotions and physical pain, and you recognize those feelings in others. Through your willingness to take on, or at least share, the pain of another, you demonstrate the best of human qualities.

Underlying the meditations in this chapter and throughout the book is the principle of limitless energy. As you go deep within yourself and then expand into limitless space, or as you use your own energy to move and align energy in another person, or as you take on the suffering of another and send back love, you realize there are no limits, no true boundaries. You can expand as far as your mind can imagine, and reach equally profound depths within yourself. The flow of energy from you to another is not limited in any way. If the ki is flowing, it is inexhaustible. Sending love to another is one certain way of attracting love to yourself.

When Physical Healing Is Not Possible

We all come to the end of this physical life. A moment arrives when no medical measures can prolong life. How can we help a dying person?

Elisabeth Kübler-Ross dedicated her life to the subject of death and dying. Through her work she discovered the profound gift of love to be given to a terminally ill patient. In her book *The Wheel of Life*, she quotes a monk: "When you sit with dying patients and children and focus on them for hours, you are in one of the highest forms of meditation."[1]

exercise

observing adults

Find time to observe people unnoticed in a public setting.

1. Sit comfortably, stand still, or walk.

2. Focus on the people around you. Observe the method in their activities. Observe repetitive patterns. Observe facial expressions as they work.

3. Observe how you feel as you watch.

---

1. Kübler-Ross, *The Wheel of Life*, 223.

Thoughts and feelings will undoubtedly arise within you as you relate to people who are unwell. The range may go from joy to sorrow and back again. The bare attention necessary for this kind of observation is a learned skill, so don't be disappointed if your attention wavers. By practicing this meditation, you learn which perceptions are about the people you observe, and which feelings and perceptions are your own. You may find that over time you are far less irritated by the actions of others. You become less judgmental of them, and more curious about what they are experiencing.

We will revisit this topic in chapter 18, "Deepening Your Spiritual Life." For now, simply try the exercise a few times and notice how it works for you.

Healing with Color

The use of color has been a part of human life ever since people learned to make paints and dyes. Even before that people probably chose to arrange and decorate their environment using colored objects. The use of color in meditation can enhance health, promote healing, and modify emotional responses.

The spiritual importance of color pervades religious art in many cultures. The Roman Catholic and Episcopal churches use different colored vestments for the liturgical seasons of the year, for holidays, and for specific services. Stained glass adorns many Christian churches. Flowers on the altar are often chosen for their spiritual color and quality.

The same is true in other religions. Hindu rituals pre-scribe certain colored clothing. Buddhist art makes use of primary colors in specific ways. American Indians assign specific colors to the four directions for spiritual reasons, and use colored sands to create paintings for healing and other purposes. The examples of the spiritual uses of color are too numerous to name.

Meditation using color can have profound effects on physical and emotional health, and can later enhance mental processes in positive ways. There are two general approaches to the use of color: One uses the full range of the color spectrum to achieve balance, nourishment, and cleansing; and the other uses a specific color to promote concentration and visualization for a specific purpose.

exercise
general color healing meditation

Sit comfortably with your eyes closed.

1. Begin slow, rhythmic breathing.

2. Visualize golden light either in front of you or over your head. As you breathe, draw the light into your body, or visualize your body moving into the light, whichever is easier.

3. Feel the light as it permeates your entire being. Feel its energy cleansing, straightening, and unblocking each limb, each organ. Feel it dissolving obstacles as it moves through you.

4. Practice this until it becomes familiar to you.

5. Repeat the exercise, now using the colors of the rainbow. You may associate the colors with the chakras mentioned in chapter 10. You may also associate the colors with how they feel to you. It generally helps to visualize the colors in the order of the rainbow: red, orange, yellow, green, blue, indigo, and violet.

6. When you have finished, visualize a radiant fountain of white light flecked with gold pouring over and through you, or surrounding you in an oval that extends above your head and beneath your feet.

You will probably find that some colors are easier to visualize than others. Notice what each color feels like. You can expect each color to feel different. Here is a list of some of the correspondences that people often experience between colors and physical or emotional feelings.

Red

Red is associated with fire and heat. Visualizing red can help increase physical feelings of warmth and the emotions of passion and anger. Red can strengthen the blood and improve circulation, and it is associated with blood and courage. The human eye is capable of discerning hundreds of shades of red, and this capacity is reflected in the many metaphors associated with this color. Your meditation on red could invoke shades from nearly orange, to pinks, cerise, cranberry, and so on. Notice the shade that you envision, and look for that color in your wardrobe and your environment.

Orange

Orange is a color associated with health. I think of carrots and oranges, which are rich in vitamins A and C. I think of carnelian beads that feel cool to the skin, no matter how hot and humid the weather. I think of sweet, juicy peaches and Rocky Ford cantaloupe. According to Bill Stuber in *Gems of the 7 Color Rays*, orange is the color to use to stimulate vitality and joy. It provides the means to balance one's physical and emotional system, and to identify what needs to change to improve one's health.[2] Meditation on the color orange will encourage a state of well being to manifest within you.

Yellow

Yellow is an active color. It is the color of the sun, of midsummer flowers, and ripe corn. It is warm, but not flaming hot. Yellow may be more difficult to sustain in meditation than other colors. This may be because when we focus on yellow, we also allow our minds to open to the vastness of the sun, and thus lose focus. The complementary side of meditating on the color yellow is the potential to ground yourself. From a solid earth connection you can experience the vastness of the sun without harm. In the midst of materiality, the color yellow opens you to the sun, the source.

---

2. Stuber, *Gems*, 143–44.

Green

Meditating on the color green deepens your connection to your inner being. We rejoice in the spring when plants burst forth and surround us with multiple shades of green. We are stimulated to fruitful action by this color. This healing color can ease the pain of grief and sorrow. It can also deepen feelings of satisfaction and remove toxic factors on the physical, mental, emotional, and spiritual levels. Meditation on green can help you achieve greater success in all activities because it establishes a closer connection between conscious action and unconscious intention.

Blue

Blue is the color of the sky, of space. Meditation on the color blue enhances your mental capacity by clearing away the distractions that invade your thoughts. When you close your eyes, it may be easier to visualize violet or indigo than blue. Thus you may want to find something blue to focus on with your eyes open. Once you have developed focus in this way, blue meditation will come more easily. Some people find that blue encourages restfulness and sleep, so don't be surprised if this meditation makes you drowsy.

Indigo

Indigo is associated with alpha brain waves, and with intuition. This color is relatively easy to visualize with eyes closed. By breathing deeply and relaxing, you will learn to evoke the color easily. By visualizing indigo, you can alter your brain waves to increase alpha waves. With practice, you can consciously will this state of mind. Many people feel rested and refreshed after this meditation. The muscles of the face and head relax. In this state a spiritual connection is made within you—you feel at peace. You will also feel more capable of accomplishing your goals.

Violet

You may find that when you meditate, particularly with your eyes closed, that you can easily visualize violet as you relax. Violet, like indigo, is often perceived when alpha brain waves are present. This color promotes the capacity to use different parts of your mind. It also creates avenues for communication without the pain associated with mental or emotional ruts. Violet can relieve headaches and other physical pains.

White

Meditation on white light is one of the most common color meditations. White light is associated with psychic protection, and with healing and wellness. Most people find it easy to imagine white light with their eyes closed. An interesting point about white light is that while it is used for protection, it does this by forming a strong connection, not by insulating against what is feared. White light is full-spectrum light, or, in other words, it integrates all the colors into one ray. This meditation stimulates the mental and sometimes moral integrity that make it possible to act selflessly.

meditation for relaxation

For most of us, relaxation is a good place to start when we seek to heal ourselves or others. We are stressed, we are tense, and we are rushing through life, seemingly with no time to just relax. As I have already pointed out, we *do* have brief moments throughout the day when we could relax, if we only learn how.

Wherever you find yourself sitting, take a two- to five-minute "time out."

1. Take a deep breath. Notice where you feel that breath in your body.

2. Now take another deep breath, but this time breathe past the point where you felt the first one.

3. Lower your eyes toward the floor, and let your eyelids drop to a comfortable position—they may actually close all the way.

4. Consciously relax your shoulders, arms, and hands, letting your hands rest on your legs or in your lap.

5. Flex muscles, arrange your feet, or arrange your body so that you are more comfortable.

6. Continue to take slow, deep breaths.

7. Come out of this brief meditation by taking a quicker breath and refocusing your eyes.

Two minutes is probably not long enough to let go of all your tension, but you will find that you are noticeably less tense. Your eyes and face may feel more rested, and your shoulders more relaxed. I often notice that my stomach and abdomen feel more "centered"—they feel like the true center of my attention.

By focusing on your own breath, you bring your attention inward. Even if you are waiting for a job interview, two minutes of this meditation will help you become more aware of what you truly want and need. Whatever the situation around you, you can always find two minutes, even if you have to escape to the restroom to do it. Focusing on yourself is an altered state of consciousness that you can enter anytime, anywhere.

_____exercise

facial relaxation

Many people carry tension in the face. You may squint, grind your teeth, or hold your mouth in a particular position for long periods of time. The tension can extend down into the neck or upward into the scalp. Many headaches are a direct result of this kind of tension.

Be sure to inhale fully and then exhale with each step of this exercise.

1. Begin your meditation as usual.

2. Taking a few deep breaths, focus your attention on your face, head, and neck.

3. Allow your eyes to close, and rest your tongue against the roof of your mouth.

4. As you breathe out, imagine that your eyes are slightly further apart. Don't use your muscles, just imagine that it happens.

5. Allow your jaw to drop slightly.

6. Imagine that your eyebrows are resting on a soft cushion.

7. Again, imagine your eyes are slightly further apart.

8. Tip your head slightly backward and forward until you find a comfortable position.

9. Imagine that your ears are slightly further back on your head.

10. Continue the deep breaths for a few moments.

11. Complete your meditation.

The mind is a powerful tool. Just imagining a change in your face allows you to relax muscles. If you have studied anatomy, you can use this meditation for specific muscles or muscle groups. The meditation can be modified for any part of the body. You may want to visualize a certain color while you are going through the steps. Adapt this relaxation exercise to suit your personal needs. You will find that you can do this exercise, or a modified version of it, just about anywhere.

Healing meditation requires practice. You may be able to achieve results quickly in some areas, and less quickly in others. All meditation practices help to achieve relaxation, a basic component of health. Focusing on healing as you meditate requires repetition to develop skill. For example, the first time you try to get your "factory workers" to help you, you may feel rather silly. You wonder the whole time if this can possibly work. After a few practice sessions, however, you will find that you indeed feel better, silly or not. The same is true of color meditations. At first they seem implausibly easy, or next to impossible. With practice you begin to feel the results in your own body or see them in the person you are helping.

The next chapter deals with the important task of finding the meditation methods that work best for you.

16

Finding What Works for You

As a result of not being attached to the outcome [of medita-
tion] a person can become completely involved in whatever
he [or she] is doing. A surprising result is that life becomes
more interesting and engaging . . .

Anonymous
"Karma Yoga: Path of Selfless Action"

AMONG THE MANY exercises presented in the
previous chapters, you have found some that seem easy,
some that seem impossible, and a few that really click with
your mind and body. You now are faced with decisions:
Which meditations should become part of my regular routine? Which ones shall I simply forget about, at least for
now? Is it all right to focus on the easy ones?

Let's begin with the last question. Where meditation is
concerned, doing what comes easily and naturally has both

a positive side and a less constructive one. As with any serious undertaking, when beginning meditation, we need to begin where we are. This means that using meditations that are simple and easy is a proper approach. For instance, it will be easier to extend the time you spend if what you are doing is not overly uncomfortable on the physical level. You will be able to sit in an easy posture, or walk on a certain path for an extended time period. This allows you to settle into the habit of spending more time in meditation.

By developing your meditation practice in this way, you may not challenge yourself very much. As you have read, there are significant challenges that arise in meditation, and it is in meeting those challenges that you grow and learn. Thus, taking the easiest path may not be the best in the long run. However, it is a fine way to get started, and a good way to build a base for future consistency.

Some of the meditations in this book are designed for rather specific purposes. It is a good idea to experiment with them when you are not in the midst of a major life challenge, so that you know how to do the meditation. For example, if you learn the practice of taking and sending (chapter 15) during a calm period of your life, you will be able to enter this meditation quickly and more easily when you are undergoing a difficult trial. Then when you are faced with the task of helping a person in great pain or turmoil, you will be able to spontaneously respond with the practice. You won't find yourself swamped by the power of the emotional reactions around you.

To take another example, the use of mantras requires practice. They can be like tongue twisters when they are repeated over and over. When teachers offer a manta in another language, they repeat it several times so that you can hear the words or syllables. Then they have you repeat it again and again, until the rhythm of the sounds is felt in the body. Only then can you say you have learned the mantra. When you begin to say it in your meditation practice, you may have to recall the situation where you learned it in order to get the proper tone and rhythm, and you may need the written words to help you; but once you have it, you can say it whenever you want or need it.

Very physical meditations may require that you develop the required strength in order to do them for the recommended length of time. Many of the more complex kundalini meditations have been omitted from this book for the very reason that they take long practice to perfect, and you may need a teacher to help you. Even the simple kundalini exercises included in chapter 10 are strenuous, and deserve careful practice to build up to the recommended times. If you have been sedentary for a long time, or if you are recuperating from an illness, even walking meditation can be a test of your strength.

Visualization requires practice both to generate the image in the first place, and to sustain the image for an extended time period. If you practice color healing meditations, you learn how to evoke the desired color more easily, and you practice maintaining that color. Later, when a situation arises that requires color healing, you already know how to evoke the color, and you can hold it in your mind more steadily. In this way your healing efforts will be very strong and potent. Without practice, you may find it difficult, if not impossible, to visualize the proper color in the moment of crisis. Your own emotional response to the situation will get in the way of the healing.

Distractions

Whether you choose the easy path or challenge yourself, you will likely be faced with days when unbidden thoughts, images, and feelings arise that interfere with your focus. These interruptions will simply not go away. Even after you have been meditating for years, there will be days when you cannot still your mind. In some ways these are the days that offer the most growth potential. It is in these moments that you are face-to-face with yourself.

Have you failed in some way? Not at all. You have grown to a new level of mind. Now you are ready for the test. Can you overcome this very familiar challenge again, now? A part of you—a little voice—says you have already dealt with this particular distraction, and chastises you for letting it get the best of you again. Another part of you—a newer, fresher voice—may say that this is how it goes, some days are better than others, and anyway, it's meditation, not a one-time offer. You will meditate again tomorrow, or later today.

It is how you face what seems like a setback that determines how you will move forward. Your meditation practice gives you little setbacks to prepare your mind to accept them in other areas of your life. Imagine! You find that you don't have to remain calm and unruffled in the face of adversity. You can be yourself for that moment—

ragged and unpolished and whatever else comes with your personal package. You can even react from instinct—whatever. What you have been learning is how to be yourself and accept your own response.

A basic belief about life is that we all do pretty much the best we can all the time. Why would you do any less? Imagine yourself taking the time to figure out the best thing to do, and then choosing to do something different—not likely. It is a fact that many actions—our own and other people's—don't look all that good. They look sloppy, uninformed, and just plain stupid. How can those be examples of the best we can do? They represent what we chose in that moment. A destructive act is a clear indication that the person doing it is in a state of confusion and suffering. The motives behind the action have been constructed on the basis of inaccurate information.

Meditation helps you to cultivate a space—a time and place—in which to make decisions. You have worked with your body and mind through practice, so you know how to tell if you are in an appropriate frame of mind to make your decision.

exercise

making decisions

Focus on a decision you need to make. It can be as simple as what to have for supper, or it can be a life-changing decision.

1. Write a few words about the choices you have developed to help focus on what you are deciding.

2. Now begin your usual meditation, sitting, walking, or whatever. Get into the rhythm of the meditation.

3. As you breathe, you may find thoughts about your decision come to you. Acknowledge them and return to your focus.

4. Do this for at least ten minutes.

Most of us agree that ten minutes is not too long to spend making a big decision. You will find that once you understand the choices, meditation can allow your body/mind to assess the choices and show you the way that feels the most satisfactory. You will identify a place in your body that feels very comfortable once you have made a choice, or you will find that an image comes to you.

Sometimes you will finish this meditation and feel as though you have not gotten the answer to your problem. That is all right. Just go about the business of the day. Later you may feel drawn quite strongly to one choice or another. The point here is to allow the choices to rest in the calm place within you that you have cultivated, instead of making the choice in the midst of turmoil. In addition, new choices may arise during your meditation. Once you have learned this technique, you will find that you feel better about most of the decisions you make, and you no longer beat yourself up for making the wrong decision. In the process, your best becomes better and better.

Combining Meditations

Some people are purists. They want to engage in one practice to the exclusion of all others. This is appropriate for some of us. Others see the richness in variety and want to get the best from different techniques. Meditation practice is no different.

You may want to take that very easy meditation—the one you can always do—and make it the cornerstone of your daily meditation. Beginning meditation by focusing on the breath is one that many people find helpful. This gets you into your body. You are aware of where the breath goes, and where it does not. You feel yourself sitting or walking. Your perceptions settle into that easy focus. You have started well.

Secondly, you may select a meditation for a specific purpose. You may have a task to perform that day, or you may know someone who can benefit from healing energy. You may have had a dream to which you can return and complete the story. If you have a physical symptom yourself, there may be a meditation that will relieve it.

A third element of your meditation is to challenge yourself. This could mean extending the time you meditate. It could involve building strength by walking longer. You could work on flexibility by holding a yoga pose or stretch. You may bring your meditative attitude to weight-lifting or any physical pursuit. You could work on developing greater compassion toward someone in your life. This part of your practice is about practical goals and working to achieve them. Sometimes this means sitting with the problem during meditation, and other times it means taking your meditative attitude to the problem.

A fourth factor in your meditation is the experience of gaps between thoughts and feelings. You have probably noticed that there are times when you are suddenly aware that you were *not* having thoughts. There is a blank moment. This gap in thoughts reveals the limitless space of mind. You are no longer totally full-up; you have moments when you don't have anything happening. During these moments, you experience the Universe and yourself in it in a new way.

You may never be able to sit down and consciously set out to experience such a gap. Rather, you sit and meditate and cultivate a relaxed frame of mind and body. You set the stage for whatever comes to you each day. Sometimes it will be the experience of profound space—the Void—and sometimes you will notice the tiny paper cut you got the day before. It is in your willingness to accept whatever comes that you develop your self-understanding.

summary

What works best for you will change over time. You may move on to more complex meditations and leave behind the simple ones. Remember that you can always return to the basics. You have learned them just as we learn to walk, talk, and eat—you won't forget. In difficult situations you may revert to the simple and familiar, using prayers, spells, or mantras as aids to connect to God, the Goddess, Universe, or Universal Mind on a level of deep familiarity.

There is time enough for the complex, and a right time to return to a simple and familiar practice.

The next chapter covers the important topic of identifying goals for your meditation practice, as well as determining when a non-goal is appropriate.

Identifying Personal Meditation Goals

Looking deeply requires courage.

Thich Nhat Hanh
The Heart of the Buddha's Teaching

ONCE YOU HAVE established your meditation practice, you may want to use it to achieve personal goals. Any goal can be pursued in this way because you are using your own mind as support group, friend, and facilitator. The reason meditation can help with setting and achieving goals is that you are aligning your conscious thought and feeling processes with your less-conscious physical and mental processes. Even if you don't focus on your spiritual nature at all, you become more aware of your mind/body connection. With a better understanding of the spiritual component of your life, you develop a powerful tool in making creative changes.

Using Meditation to Quit Smoking or Eliminate Any Drug Habit

If you have made a decision to quit smoking or to face some other drug habit, you have already invested considerable time and effort in thinking about the logical reasons why you should do this. You may have already tried to quit with some degree of success, but now find that you need to marshal greater personal resources in order to be fully successful. You may have been self-critical when you relapsed. You wonder why you can't just stop, and you experience both physical and emotional pain.

Meditation by itself may not be the whole solution to your addiction. You may need medical help to withdraw from drugs, for example. You may find that individual or group counseling is very helpful. You may follow a twelve-step program. Meditation, however, can provide the additional source of determination and conviction for which you have been searching. There are several reasons why meditation helps you break smoking or drug habits:

- **The breath cleanses the physical body.** Through meditation you learn to breathe deeply and rhythmically. As you extend your meditation from a few minutes to longer sessions, you are bringing cleansing energy into your lungs and circulatory system. Whether you are sitting or doing a moving meditation, you are using spans of time to clear toxins from your system. Deep breathing expands your lung capacity so that you bring in more clean air with each breath you take.

- **You make friends with yourself.** In previous chapters you have read about making friends with yourself through meditation. You have seen how you allow thoughts to arise, and you return to your focus. You have tried numerous exercises that reveal your typical thought processes, both creative and less constructive. You have learned to accept these processes as part of your whole being. You have discovered colors that enhance your meditative state, and you have even laughed out loud in meditation.

- **You develop other, better choices of behavior.** Acceptance is an essential step toward mastery of any addiction. The next step is to develop alternatives—other choices for behavior that can replace the habit with something more wholesome and creative. You have already established the simple act of breathing as one such behavior.

- **The breath clears the mind.** You have used the breath as a focus in meditation. You can carry this focus into your daily life. Whenever you feel a desire for a cigarette or for some other substance, stop and take at least three deep breaths as you do in meditation. You will find that three deep, full breaths are enough to get you past a momentary craving. The breath is a natural way of nourishing your body and your mind. Deep breaths expand the chest, stretch muscles that may feel constricted, and improve posture. Deep breathing slows the heart rate by increasing the available oxygen.

Three deep breaths allow you to move from a destructive thought to a creative thought. You interrupt the addictive pattern with this breathing technique. Each new behavior you develop through this exercise provides another way to interrupt the destructive behavior you seek to change. Soon you have an arsenal of weapons in your fight, and eventually there is no fight because you cease to struggle against your former enemy.

exercise

gaining insight into the mechanism of the habit

You have to learn how your addiction functions so you can overcome it. Through understanding you can find the creative choices that replace the addictive behavior.

1. Begin your meditation as usual.

2. Breathe deeply and rhythmically, and relax into a comfortable meditation.

3. Allow your addiction to become the focus of your awareness. Let your awareness examine every aspect of the addiction. How do you obtain the substance? When do you use it? How does it feel in your hands, your mouth, your system?

4. Recall an especially satisfying time when you were smoking or using.

5. Continue your exploration. Notice the less pleasant facets of the addiction. Is there an unpleasant smell? Do you feel weak or nauseated? Do you worry about how expensive the habit is?

6. Notice the color that you experience most often when you are using or smoking. How does it differ from the colors you can visualize during meditation? As you focus on the color, how does it change?

7. Focus on your breathing for a few moments, and then look at the color again. How is it different?

The goal of this exercise is to help you make friends with your addiction. Yes, you have seen it as a friend in the past, but that friend has become a difficult, limiting, even harmful acquaintance. Now you become friends in the sense that you understand the addictive behavior as a part of your life, and a part of yourself. You accept it as a reality instead of denying it.

---

e x e r c i s e

creating new behaviors

You may have identified new behaviors that you want to learn and practice. If not, you can use meditation to help you discover new ways of satisfying the needs and desires that have been part of your addiction. You may want to make a list of the reasons (excuses?) for your addictive behavior. Perhaps you smoke when you are hanging out with friends. Perhaps you use an addictive substance to lessen pain. Perhaps you like the speedy feeling you get from particular drugs. Make another list of the downsides of your behavior. Perhaps you spend all your disposable income and more on the habit. You alienate friends and family with your behavior. You harm your physical and mental health. Your time is consumed by the addictive behavior when you could be doing something more constructive, more creative, more fun. Take these lists into the meditation exercise.

1. Begin your meditation as usual.

2. As you settle into the breath and focus your mind, recall the positive and negative items you have listed.

3. Focus on each item on your list. Allow thoughts to arise. These may come in the form of colors, words, images, or physical feelings. Ask for suggestions for new creative activities to replace the addictive behavior. Remember to ask for behaviors that you can actually do. If you are focusing on hanging out with friends, ask for a hanging out behavior that replaces smoking or other habits.

4. Whatever ideas arise, don't discount them. They may seem silly or even downright weird. Still, they are ideas that have emerged from within your consciousness. Add them to a new written list of alternatives. If an idea arises that you are pretty sure you cannot do because of physical or other limitations, focus on

that idea and notice what thought arises about how to modify it into something you can do. For example, you cannot fly to the moon, but you can go to the planetarium. Most of us cannot perform extreme gymnastics or other sports activities, but we can do simple yoga or play catch with our friends.

5. If you have long lists of positive and less-constructive facets of your addictive behavior, you may need to consider them in several meditation sessions. There is really no rush with this exercise. You can explore your behavior at a comfortable pace.

In the beginning you may find that your smoking or addictive behavior seems to be worse. By focusing on it you bring it right into your face, so to speak. When this happens, you now have at least two choices. One is to pursue your habit. Another is to return to your meditation. Still more choices may have emerged from this exercise. The point is, *you have choices.* As you work with this and other exercises, you will develop more choices. Any time you feel the addictive urge, you can choose to do something else.

I am not recommending that you deny the addictive choice. You know you can do it because you have been doing it. I recommend that you also recognize your other choices, and enumerate their benefits to you. You can choose to do other things more and more often. Eventually you will come to the point where other choices are more attractive than the addictive choices.

In writing about this exercise, I felt a sharp pain in my upper chest. At first I didn't recognize it. I stopped writing, sat in a relaxed posture, and began the deep breathing of meditation. After a few moments, I recognized the pain. It was the pain from coughing—the muscle constriction that occurred with smoker's cough. I hardly remember that pain, it has been so long since I felt it. I have successfully replaced my smoking behavior with the capacity to breathe fully and freely.

If you have engaged in an addictive behavior for an extended period of time, you will need some time to recover. Most addictions cause physical symptoms, as well as mental and emotional harm. Meditation can provide a safe environment in which to explore the addiction and its harmful impact on you. Step by step, you can replace the negatives with positive behaviors that you consciously control. You can also use meditation to heal the symptoms themselves.

Weight Loss and Meditation

Some people have suggested that eating is also an addiction. I find that this view is not at all helpful. It is one thing to recover from an addiction to something you truly don't need in your life, but it is another thing to try to eliminate food. We have to nourish our bodies in order to be healthy, and we do that with food. The problems with food are choosing those that are good for you, and choosing appropriate quantities. Weight loss has other components as well. Exercise appropriate to your age and general physical health is known to be helpful in any weight-loss program. You need to have minerals and vitamins in your daily diet to maintain physical health. You even need enough fat in your diet to absorb fat-soluble vitamins.

Food allergies may hamper weight-loss efforts. This may be because when you eat something you are allergic to, the body provides signals that you need something else to counter the allergy. It may be that the allergic reaction includes the desire for more of that substance. It may be that the allergic reaction interferes with digestion and assimilation. The details of these possibilities are beyond the scope of this meditation book. (For more information, consult with a physician or alternative health practitioner to determine how allergies may be affecting your weight and overall health. See also the books by Braly and Rivera in the bibliography.)

Metabolic rate has been proven to affect how the body uses energy. The body is designed to conserve energy and use it effectively. If metabolism is slow, the food you consume is stored as fat. If your metabolic rate is higher, more energy is used, and thus less is stored. So how can meditation help with weight loss? There are several ways:

- Meditation can help you to focus on your weight-loss goal. You can align your conscious goal with your internal, less-conscious goals.

- You can identify alternative behaviors that replace eating when you are not hungry, or that satisfy the hunger signals you receive.

- Moving meditation provides exercise. You can begin with simple movements for a few minutes, and increase to longer, more complex, moving meditations. Walking meditation gets you moving too. As you meditate for longer periods, you walk more—very simple.

- You can become more aware of the effect different foods have on your mood, your body, and your thought process. Through conscious observation—a skill cultivated through meditation—you discover which foods truly satisfy you, which ones only satisfy for a short time, and which ones satisfy some need other than hunger. An example is the desire to bite down and chew. This can be satisfied with carrots or beef jerky instead of potato chips, which have more salt and fat than you need.

- You develop choices that satisfy mental, emotional, and even spiritual hunger in ways that don't involve eating. Meditation has proven to be very satisfying in itself. Remember, you meditate for yourself, not for anyone else. It is quality time you spend with yourself. Through meditation you discover other choices.

- Eventually you learn which foods to avoid. I use the term "avoid" because you don't have to give them up completely. You can taste them now and then. You can save them for special occasions.

- By paying close attention, you learn how much of something will satisfy your desire. For example, allowing one small square of chocolate to melt in your mouth can be as satisfying as gobbling an entire candy bar.

reviewing meditation options

Instead of providing a specific exercise here, I want you to look back over the exercises in the book. Recall the ones you have tried. Experiment with ones you have not yet tried.

1. Notice which exercises come easily.

2. Notice which meditations leave you feeling relaxed, rested, and comfortable.

3. Notice any that agitate you or make you uncomfortable.

4. Find a moving meditation that suits your circumstances, and make it part of your daily routine.

5. Find a visualization that is consistent with your weight-loss goal. Create an intermediate weight-loss goal that feels doable. Remember from the exercise in this chapter that whatever choices you create, they must be something you can actually do.

The goal here is to develop meditations that support your personal goals, whatever they may be. Meditation helps to align the conscious goals with your less-conscious process. In this way your whole being is headed toward the same goal.

Your meditation can be focused on a particular goal, and consistent meditation will help you achieve goals in every area of your life. Meditation also can help with non-goals. Perhaps you are all too driven in your daily life. In fact, you may have decided at some point in the past that meditation was a big waste of time for you. Meditation can be an activity that is not goal oriented. The non-goal, if you will, is to simply meditate without expectation.

We have looked at some physical values found in meditation. In the next chapter, meditation is considered as a factor in your spiritual life.

18

Deepening Your Spiritual Life

True compassion is not just an emotional response but a firm commitment founded on reason. Therefore, a truly compassionate attitude toward others does not change even if they behave negatively.

His Holiness the Dalai Lama
The Path to Tranquility

YOU MAY FIND that when you meditate, a particular person frequently comes into your thoughts. It could be a family member, a friend—anyone you have feelings about. If the feelings are positive, you will naturally take a moment to enjoy the experience. If the feelings are not so positive, you may try to distract yourself from the experience. In both cases you have been drawn away from meditation itself into a thought process.

After examining your feelings, good or bad, you find that you can settle back into your meditation more easily. In the case of a person who feels good to you, nothing much needs to be done. In the case of someone who causes negative feelings, you can benefit from understanding the dynamic of the relationship. Some people think forgiveness and compassion are platitudes. This meditation helps you to substitute a more positive feeling for a negative one in a way that changes your mental habits for the better.

exercise

exercise in compassion I

This exercise has three parts: a part in which you are just thinking about the process, a part where you actively engage the process, and a part where you practice compassion for whatever arises in your mind. The following is the first part.

1. In your mind, identify a person toward whom you feel some resentment or anger.

2. Think about that individual and whatever has happened to cause you to feel the way you do.

3. Try not to judge your feelings—just observe them. Not fun, yet most of us spend considerable amounts of time in just such negative thought processes. Now you have an opportunity to change that process.

4. Prepare yourself to meditate.

5. Begin steady rhythmic breathing.

6. As you relax, envision something that has good thoughts and feelings associated with it. It could be an open space, a flower, or a symbol. Allow time to find a particularly powerful symbol.

7. As you focus on this object, notice the feeling of warmth that surrounds you. Notice the colors you associate with this feeling.

8. Now think of the problem individual. Alternate thoughts of that individual with your chosen "good feeling" object. Now the problem person, now the good feeling, now the problem, now the good feeling.

9. Continue for several minutes.

Notice now, as you think about that person, that hints of good feelings tend to slip into your awareness. This may be very subtle. As we change the thoughts and feelings we associate with an experience, our minds change. As you practice the technique you will find that it happens more quickly and easily. Some negative thoughts change more easily than others. Some require an intense commitment. Some even seem impossible to change.

His Holiness the Dalai Lama compares meditation to other growth processes:

In the case of a small child, the child has to grow up into a well-built young [person], but the growth takes place with the passage of time. It cannot happen overnight. Likewise the transformation of mind will also take time.[1]

exercise in compassion II

1. Prepare to meditate.

2. Begin steady breathing, and focus your thoughts on something for which you feel compassion. Perhaps it is a kitten or puppy that needs your warmth and love. Perhaps it is a sick friend or family member who has asked for your help. Perhaps you feel compassion for the survivors of an earthquake. Generally compassion is associated with another living thing, but you may find that the earth itself is worthy of your positive feelings.

3. Focus on your object of compassion for a few minutes. Consider what inspires your feelings about this person or thing.

4. Continue for a few minutes, allowing yourself to rest in the feelings you associate with compassionate thoughts.

Notice that you feel different in some way after this brief experience. You remember the details of the kitten's face and how it plays. You remember how much better you

---

1. Dalai Lama, *The Path to Tranquility*, 311.

feel when your sick friend is able to relax and go to sleep. You remember a small action that makes you feel like you are doing your part for the planet. Spend some time with this feeling of compassion so you can more easily recall how it feels.

exercise in compassion III

1. Prepare to meditate again.

2. As you breathe, focus on the meditation.

3. Allow whatever thoughts you have to occur.

4. When you observe a thought about anything, associate that thought with the feelings of compassion that you have. Do this for whatever thoughts or feelings arise.

5. Continue for ten minutes or longer.

Notice how this process feels different from other meditation experiences. Did many thoughts and feelings arise? Were you able to stay focused on one thought for an extended period as you associated compassionate thoughts and feelings with it? How does this seemingly simple process change how you feel toward your own mental process?

The healing capacity of compassion is immense. You are capable of experiencing this feeling moment to moment if you practice it. Most of us have negative thoughts from time to time that we don't really need. Replacing them with something more positive helps us and helps the people around us as well. We find that we like other people more, and that they like us too. We find that we appreciate everyday experiences more. Finally, we find that we engage in each experience more directly as we seek to discover what there is to enjoy about it.

The Dalai Lama describes compassionate thought in the following way:

> You have to understand that the affection I am speaking of has no purpose, it is not given with the intention of getting anything back. It is not a matter of feeling. In the same way we say that real compassion is without attachment. Pay attention to this point, which goes against our habitual ways of thinking. It is not this or that particular case that stirs our pity. We don't give our compassion to such and such a person by choice. We give it spontaneously, entirely, without hoping for anything in exchange. And we give it universally.[2]

Thinking back to the individual who provokes irritation in you, notice how that individual is among the potential objects of your compassion. If you are unable to feel compassion toward this person, you may want to avoid him or her and cultivate compassion in a more suitable setting. Then when you see the person later, you may find that your feelings of irritation occur less frequently or less intensely. Acknowledge that this individual is very diffi-

---

2. Ibid., 385.

cult for you to like. In this way you have compassion for yourself. If you give compassion spontaneously and universally, you surely include yourself as well.

In chapter 15, "Healing Meditation," the principles of ki meditation and taking and sending meditation were introduced. In ki meditation you practiced expanding your awareness outward from yourself to include the room, the building, the neighborhood, the planet, the solar system, and even the whole Universe. You also tried going deep within yourself, experiencing the sounds, movements, and feelings inside your body. As you practice this meditation—moving out and moving back to yourself—you will relate to the world in a different way. Instead of feeling separate from everything, you begin to feel at one with it. It is easy to feel compassion for those things that are one with you.

Taking and sending meditation is based on compassion from the very start. The act of taking on the suffering of another is good practice for taking on your own suffering. If you can take on suffering for another, and if you find greater calm and peace in so doing, then you can do the same for yourself. By saying, "I take on my pain in this moment," you face it clearly. By facing it, you don't have to ignore it, only to face it again later. By facing suffering, we don't necessarily eliminate pain, but we do deal with the pain in a whole new way.

I recall a situation in which my granddaughter accidentally swallowed some medicine that could have caused her great harm. Her parents rushed her to the hospital, where they immediately began treatment. Part of the treatment involved taking frequent blood samples. This whole experience was intensely frightening and painful (and would have been for an adult!). Her father, feeling the compassion that anyone would feel, couldn't do anything to solve the medical problem. What he did instead was to hold her and repeat her own mantra, "Owee, owee, it hurts! It hurts!" He shared her experience and helped her to feel less alone.

---

summary

Do not underestimate the power of compassion and love in your life. You may not be capable of moving a physical mountain, but with love and compassion you can move mountains of troubles out of your path, and you can clear a path for others as well. Compassion enlivens your experience and replaces deadening thoughts and feelings.

Building upon what you have learned about compassion, the next chapter addresses your creative process and how to become more creative.

19

Mapping Your Personal Creative Process

You are getting continual messages from your unconscious mind. Your unconscious mind is the source of your personal creativity.

Dawna Markova
The Open Mind

AFTER YOU HAVE practiced meditation for a while, you begin to see patterns in your mental processes. Among the scattered thoughts that arise you will find groupings that begin to reveal not only what distracts you from creativity, but also the pattern of creativity itself.

The first type of repetitive distractions relates to specific issues that you are dealing with on a day-to-day basis. You may be trying to complete school or work projects and the details keep slipping away from you, so you find yourself thinking about the problem throughout your meditation.

You may have a relationship problem that seems to be constantly on your mind. Whatever the distraction, it comes up again and again as you meditate. This type of thinking is dependent on your current life situation.

Another kind of distraction is one that will arise regardless of the current situation. This pattern of thinking relates to your life as a whole. Often it begins to come up only after you have quieted those distractions related to day-to-day living. This pattern of thinking often relates to existential questions; you ponder the same thoughts in your meditation that you often consider in conversations with friends, or in private moments when you think about the meaning of life. An example of this kind of thinking is repetitive concerns about people starving in Africa and the associated idea of suffering. You feel sympathy, compassion, or deep concern when you have this type of thought.

There are several ways to work with your distractions to understand the creative process within or behind them. As a thought arises again and again, you will perceive the direction you tend to go with. The personal thought about a relationship will change over time. Each time you have the thought, you will notice subtle nuances that may or may not reflect changes in the relationship. These changes may be the result of your mind working creatively to solve a problem or move the relationship to a new level.

When an existential series of thoughts arises, you may find yourself following a path toward despair—you feel you cannot do anything to solve the problem. After a while, though, you find that despair gives way to thoughts about what you *can* do. You may not be able to solve the food shortage in Africa, but you can talk about the problem, write to your state representative, and so on. You can have compassionate thoughts for those people, and your compassion will spread to the people around you. Continuing to meditate allows the second layer of thoughts to arise.

Another thing you will begin to notice is how you are able to come back to your meditation focus. You find that you do come back to your focus, sometimes quickly and sometimes slowly. You will also discover *how* this works. What happens to remind you that you are supposed to be meditating? Is it the little twinge in your knee from sitting still so long? Is it that you discover you have been holding your breath? What are the signals that bring you back to your focus? Once you identify these cues, you will find that they come into your awareness more easily. You are then able to return to your focus sooner.

Another insight that occurs relates to what feels easy or difficult. Some days, just getting to your meditation space is hard. You are distracted by anything and everything in your path. It is important to get there and to sit, even if it is only for a few minutes. Even if you are distracted the entire time and barely able to begin your meditation, you have honored your commitment by trying. Remember, not every meditation session will be ideal. Part of what you are doing is learning to work with your own mental and emotional processes, which, you can be certain, are not consistent. Notice what is hard and what is easy, and notice what happens when you focus on either.

Sometimes you will challenge yourself by facing a difficulty in your meditation. Notice what happens when you push in a difficult direction. How is the problem affected when you make it the focus of your attention? What does it look like, feel like, or smell like? Examine its attributes in detail. You may find that you even make friends with the problem. It is a part of your life, at least temporarily, and you can approach it as you would a friend, asking the problem itself to speak to you. In this way you gain information about why it is nagging you. This information can be a formidable creative ally.

As you examine a series of distractions to your meditation, you will learn about how you perceive boundaries. To begin with, meditation has its own boundaries. You have decided what constitutes a suitable place for meditation, for example. If the space becomes overly important, you may not be able to meditate in other situations. This limitation is a kind of boundary. You may find, when doing color meditations, that a certain color is very difficult to evoke. That represents a boundary to your mental process. Finally, you may find that one particular distraction is relentless.

How you perceive boundaries or limitations in meditation is a good indicator of how you see limitations in your daily life. You may have a characteristic way of thinking about problems when they arise. For example, when you don't immediately get your way in an argument, do you tend to think the other person is being mean to you, or that he or she is arguing for the sake of argument? Perhaps you are usually able to put the problem into its proper context, but occasionally certain kinds of arguments push your buttons. The feelings that come up in meditation are basically the same feelings you tend to have in other activities.

When you think through a problem and try to make a plan to solve it, you have a typical mental process that you use. This same process occurs during meditation. As you sit and practice, you will begin to see what your pattern of thought is like, and then you will be able to change it. As you change the pattern in your meditation, you will see comparable changes in other situations. Your mental approach will become calmer and steadier—not totally consistent, perhaps, but more flexible on average.

Meditation points out the physical limitations of your body. Some people will never be able to sit in lotus position for one minute, never mind for an hour of meditation. Others find this posture simple. Some people find that a foot goes to sleep, or that a particular muscle never seems to quite relax. You may have a little catch in your breathing when you try to slow it down. The physical challenges of daily life may pervade your typical distractions, and this will be reflected in some way in your meditation.

We all experience emotional walls that we have erected to protect ourselves from pain. These tend to be a less-conscious part of daily life—they are there, but we don't think about them. Meditation will present these obstacles for your consideration. It is important to treat emotional responses as friends. You have cultivated these responses for security reasons. They have served a positive purpose in your life. If they no longer seem positive, now is the time to add a more creative set of responses so that you can choose a different emotional avenue. Keep the old response for the occasions when it is just the right one. Practice new responses in your meditation so they also will be available in your daily life.

Many of us have so little spare time that we hardly ever consider spiritual matters at all. There is the mother of five children who spends every waking moment feeding, clothing, washing, and otherwise dealing with her family. There is the businessman who is busy sixteen hours a day with business deals. He goes to church one hour a week and that's about it for spiritual considerations. Meditation provides the quiet environment for spiritual matters to come into consciousness. Earlier in this chapter the subject of people starving in Africa was mentioned. When such a thought enters your meditation, you may find that you go on to explore your spiritual beliefs concerning suffering. In fact, any distraction, if pursued, may lead to spiritual considerations.

All of the distractions mentioned here, and more, provide the possibility for you to accept your attitudes and feelings. You learn to accept the so-called bad thoughts as well as the good. They are, after all, just thoughts. You learn to label them and go back to your meditation. You learn to pursue them (either during your meditation time or at another time), work with them, and make friends with them, becoming consciously familiar with mental activities that previously were largely unconscious.

With conscious awareness comes the possibility for creative change. Take the example of a mathematical problem. You have to understand the components of the problem in order to find the solution. To add 398 and 144, you have to understand what the numbers mean. Then you can find the sum.

Most of life's problems do not have a unique solution. Some part of us would like to think there is one true, right, best solution in every case, but that just isn't how life works. Meditation aids the creative process by cultivating different responses—different ways to solve problems. You are able to work with a problem, find a number of choices for how to solve it, and then take action. The frustration and fear that accompany indecision are greatly lessened when you have a practiced method in place for developing choices.

summary

This chapter has considered ways for you to understand your unique internal processes, and to discover the creative capacity within yourself. The capacity for making well-informed choices is part of the foundation for your creative process. The abilities developed in meditation are the cornerstones upon which you build your life skills. Through understanding your unique creative process, you prepare yourself for whatever ups and downs come into your life.

The next chapter deals with the seemingly simple task of naming things and ideas, and how this task is integral to meditation.

20

Labeling

Whatsoever things are objects of sight, hearing, and experience—these things I hold in higher esteem.

Heraclitus
Fragments

BY THIS POINT in the book you have tried some different exercises, and you have discovered something about how you are distracted from your meditation. Certain specific thoughts or types of thoughts come up over and over again as you concentrate on your breath, an object, or a movement. You have learned about the sorts of things that distract you from your daily living experience as well.

You have also probably discovered that you cannot stop these particular thoughts or feelings from arising. They come unbidden. Sometimes they are only vague impressions. One way to work with these thoughts is to label or name them.

Labeling

Naming is one of the first things we learn as children. Before we learned how to talk, we learned the names of hundreds of things: the parts of the body, different kinds of food, articles of clothing, the names of people in our lives. We learned words for doing things. Children clearly understand what is said to them months before they learn to speak the words. They enjoy stories and are willing to listen to them again and again.

Your meditation is similar. Particular thoughts arise again and again for you to observe them. You have the same feelings again and again. Perhaps you wonder where they come from, or perhaps you wish they would go away. Yet they don't stop.

Just as the small child is intrigued by the names of things, you can use your innate curiosity to help in the meditation process. When a thought, image, or feeling continues to arise, you may want to label it. At first you may simply label every distraction as "thinking." After all, the process of thinking is exactly what is happening. Thoughts are arising.

As you spend time practicing your chosen meditation, you notice that the same or similar thoughts recur. When you notice that you have thoughts about the same problem—paying the bills, for example—you can label this thought "paying bills." If an emotion arises, such as sadness, you can name it. If an image comes repeatedly to you, label it. By naming your thoughts, you accomplish two things: You recognize and honor your own thinking process, and you anchor the thought so that it is not quite so insistent.

naming thoughts

1. Prepare yourself for meditation in your preferred way.

2. Have paper and pen close by, in case you decide you need to make a note of anything.

3. Begin your meditation, breathing rhythmically.

4. Notice when you are distracted, and identify that you are distracted.

5. As you are distracted, name the kind of distraction. Instead of simply returning to your focus, label the thought, feeling, or image.

6. Continue for ten minutes or more.

What did you notice about the pattern of your thoughts? Do you tend to be distracted by the same thing over and over, or are your distractions seemingly random? Did your meditation change when you began the labeling process?

exercise

following thoughts

Now that you have tried naming during your meditation, the next step is to go with whatever thought arises. This sounds easy, but you will find it takes some interesting turns.

1. Prepare for your meditation as usual.

2. Remember the paper and pen.

3. Begin your meditation. Allow yourself to relax into the typical rhythm of breathing.

4. When a thought comes to you, name it.

5. Then, instead of going back to the breath, follow the thought for a few moments. Focus on it. If it is about paying the bills, focus on this thought. What bills need to be paid? How much money is involved? Go over the steps of bill paying in your mind: getting out the checkbook, finding the bill you received in the mail, determining the amount, writing the check, recording the check for your own records, putting the payment stub and check into the envelope, sealing it, adding a stamp, putting it in the mail. Try to get as much detail as you possibly can about the thought, feeling, or image that you are following.

6. Notice what other random thoughts or feelings arose while you were engaged in this focused process. Label them and go back to the process on which you are focusing.

7. Do this for ten minutes or more.

What do you notice about the distraction you were pursuing? Have your feelings changed toward this subject? Were you able to focus and explore all the facets of the distraction? Do you now know enough to handle that distraction the next time it arises? What additional information do you need on the subject?

The point of these exercises is not to make particular distractions go away, because they won't. The object is to train your mind to stay with a subject even if it is something you would prefer to avoid. Paying bills was chosen as an example because it is not a favorite activity for most of us. By the same token, if we can be mindful—if we can focus on this process and do it fully and well—we find that bill-paying is a task that can be completed within a few moments. We cease to allow it to worry us all the time.

Something similar happens with feelings. When you have learned this kind of focused attention, you are able to deal with situations when they arise in your life, so that you don't have worries left over to disturb your concentration, or your meditation. As you develop this skill, your confidence level improves. You know you are capable of dealing with events and feelings, instead of being overwhelmed by them.

This meditation is a good one to do about once a week. At first you can practice it more often to learn how it works, and then do it only when you want to sort out a specific problem.

_____s u m m a r y

The ability to name things is such a fundamental skill that we seldom think about it in our daily activities. The first language tasks for infants include learning to associate sounds with the names of people and things, and language is the vehicle for computation and abstract thought. By occasionally returning to this simple task of naming, you return to one of the basic components of mind.

The next chapter carries this concept of simplicity into the creation of a space dedicated to meditation.

21

Creating a
Meditation Space

Breathing, you invisible poem!
World-space constantly in pure
Interchange with our own being. Counterpoise,
Wherein I rhythmically happen.

Rainer Maria Rilke
Sonnets to Orpheus

AS YOU GAIN experience with meditation, you
may want to develop a space that is more or less dedicated to
meditation. Most people find that it is easier to meditate in
a space that is not filled with noise and visual distractions.
In addition, certain objects become associated with the
practice of meditation and make it easier to engage in your
practice.

As was stated at the beginning of this book, you need
very little to begin meditating. Mostly you need a few

minutes each day and the intention to learn how to focus and calm your mind and body. However, a meditation space can be very beneficial. You can reflect on the places that have been conducive to your meditation. The colors, furniture, sounds, odors, even the temperature and degree of light all affect your ability to concentrate. Below you'll find a few items that may initially be useful.

Cushion or Chair

Because you must be reasonably comfortable to begin meditating, most people need a floor covering, at least, and a cushion or chair on which to sit. If you are flexible enough to sit in lotus posture, that is good. If you are not, then sitting on a firm cushion, stool, or even a chair can be helpful. The seat should be firm and steady so that you feel secure. When you sit, you are using gravity to anchor yourself comfortably. If you sit in a chair, place both feet flat on the floor. Whatever you do, sit with your spine erect, and find a balanced position so that you don't have to work hard to stay upright. If you choose to meditate while lying on your back, support your lower spine with a small pillow or rolled towel to relieve stress.

Table or Shrine

You may wish to create a table, altar, or shrine on which you place objects that have special meaning for you. If you have a particular religious bent, you may choose statues, pictures, or religious implements to adorn your shrine. Churches, mosques, and temples of all kinds are usually decorated to inspire certain feelings and thoughts, and your meditation space is no different. Traditional shrines are designed to serve as inspiration for a wide range of individuals. Your personal shrine needs only to help you in your daily practice of meditation, so it can look as different as you want.

In creating any ritual space, it is important to incorporate the four elements: fire, earth, air, and water. This does not mean that you have to have lighted candles, a fan blowing, or anything specific. However, some representation of the four elements helps to establish balance in a space. For example, seashells can replace actual water. A gong or bell reminds one of the air that carries the sound, and statues and other objects convey the sense of earth. Burning incense conveys the sense of air. Candles are an easy way to incorporate fire, but they require care to avoid larger fires when the candle burns down or when the flame is blown into combustible materials.

Wall Decorations

Images and patterns can be used to decorate the walls in your shrine space. These can range from postcard-sized pictures of animals or outdoor spaces to wall-sized Buddhist thangkas (paintings). The idea here is to convey a sense of the sacred.

Meditation can become a spiritual practice for you, or it can remain a simple relaxation technique. Thus you can choose to decorate the space to suit your personal desires. Many people start out with very personalized décor and drift toward more traditional designs. Others find personal touches that make the meditation experience more profound. You determine what your own sacred space is all about.

Because you are working with space, the meditation area by definition should convey a sense of spaciousness. This doesn't mean you have to dedicate an entire room to meditation, although you may want to do so. It does mean that you have to be far enough away from the walls so you don't feel crowded. The shrine should be far enough away that the smell of burning incense is not too intense, and the shrine itself is not a distraction. Any shrine decorations should be consistent with the space available.

Before you spend a lot of money on decorations for your shrine, you may want to develop your meditation practice a bit. What initially seems calming may shift over time. Images that seem rather garish or dreadful at first may become more attractive as you spend time in your meditation space. Buddhist art is composed of bright colors and metallic gold touches. Western churches are decorated with seasonal colors to remind the churchgoer of the cycle of the year. Mosques have intricate design work in the decorations. The range of possibilities is endless, and you have lots of time to decide what works best for you. Understand the space itself first. Then decide what furnishings will suit it best.

Consider what is behind you as you are sitting. You may seat yourself with a wall close behind, or you may be closer to the center of the space. Many people are uncomfortable with their backs to the doorway, so you may want to either face the door, or have it in your peripheral vision. The same is true for windows—the light may be more comfortable coming from a particular direction. If you meditate at night, there should be adequate light so that you are comfortable in the space, unless you are using the darkness itself for a specific purpose.

If you decide to redecorate your meditation space, be respectful of the objects you remove. Dispose of them properly, store them carefully, or give them to someone who can put them to good use. By doing this, you maintain your positive attitude toward meditation and your meditation space.

_____exercise

experiencing ordinary spaces

As you move about in the world, pay attention to the spaces you move through. How do they feel? Are the feelings appropriate to the purpose of the space? If not, why not? What would you change to make the space more comfortable? How does what you learn about space affect your meditation and its space?

_____exercise

experiencing sacred spaces

Visit churches and meditation halls. Walk around the space, both indoors and outdoors. Get a feel for the shapes, the colors, and the various adornments. Sit quietly for a while to experience the space.

While most meditation spaces have characteristics in common, what works best for you personally may include unique elements. Your space does not have to be expensive or fancy to provide an atmosphere conducive to meditation. With practice, you discover that certain things help you, like a comfortable chair or cushion. Other things distract you, such as very bright light or loud music. By spending time in different meditative environments, you will develop a sense of what works best for you, and can then decorate your meditation space accordingly.

The following chapter deals with the desire to attract your life partner through meditation.

22

Soul Mate Meditation

> *How shall I withhold my soul so that it does not touch on*
> *yours?*
> *. . . Everything that touches us, you and me,*
> *takes us together . . .*

Rainer Maria Rilke
Translations

MANY OF US are seeking our soul mates. We want to have that one relationship of perfect love and friendship that will fulfill our dreams, and we may wonder how best to find such a partner.

Meditation first explores who you are. If you have tried some of the earlier meditation exercises, you have no doubt discovered quite a bit about your own mind and how it works. You have found meditations that are relaxing, calming, and restful, and you have probably found some that you don't even want to try. You have begun your self-exploration.

Because finding a loving partner is one of your primary goals, it is reasonable to think that meditation may help you. This chapter provides ways to use meditation to discover what your perfect partner is like, and how to open yourself to the experience of a soul mate relationship. In the process you will look at your own deficiencies and strengths.

exercise

contemplating your soul mate ideal

1. Begin your meditation as usual.

2. As you breathe deeply and relax, hold the thought of a soul mate in your mind.

3. What thoughts arise as you focus on this idea?

4. Follow those thoughts for a few moments.

5. Consider whatever comes to you, even if it seems not to relate to a soul mate in any way.

6. Continue for a few minutes.

7. Now stop and make a few notes about what you just experienced. Write down the symbols, colors, feelings—whatever you experienced. Don't worry if it doesn't make sense.

Your notes represent information from deeper within you. Because you are focusing on your ideal soul mate, whatever you experienced relates in some way. Some of it doesn't make sense now, some of it won't make sense until you meet your soul mate, and some of it may never make sense. Still, you wrote it down as part of this exercise, and you can keep your notes for future reference.

You may want very specific information. What does he or she look like? What is his or her profession? Where does this person live? Consider what came to you in the meditation with regard to each of your questions. Some of the details may begin to make more sense.

Opening to Your Soul Mate

A second benefit of your meditation practice is that you become more open to the possibility of being deeply loved. After all, you are examining your own mind. You are finding out that you have some limitations, and you are also learning to love yourself anyway. As you develop this unconditional positive regard for yourself, you have experienced growing compassion for others. Other people can feel this expression of compassion. You are able to let other people know that you are open.

As you open, you are also able to project your physical desire in a conscious way. You may have expressed such desire before, but now it is much more conscious. You are able to moderate it, instead of being totally under its control. You can also surrender to it at the appropriate time.

exercise

experiencing desire

1. Begin your meditation as usual.

215

2. As you relax, focus on any physical desire within you. You may simply desire to shift your position, or to scratch an itch. Stay with your focus on desire. Allow your attention to enter different parts of your body. Notice where desire is found. Don't be surprised if it is in your foot or your shoulder. Be open to what you find.

3. Complete your meditation.

You may already know a lot about your own desires, and this meditation may bring no surprises. You may find that desire is all about the touch of breath on your hand just before it is kissed, or the feeling when someone is close behind you, supporting you, or the feel and taste of a small chocolate in your mouth. Some of what you find does not require a soul mate for fulfillment—you can put the chocolate in your mouth, after all—but some of what you experience may require another person to make it whole. It is in these discoveries that you learn what a soul mate can be.

Take what you have learned with you out into the world. Watch other people as they go about their business. You will soon see that some of them act in ways that are consistent with what you know about your desires. Others are nowhere close. You are learning how to identify people who are closer to your ideal, and those who miss the mark by quite a bit. Instead of depending on other people to convince you they are right, you are looking for "rightness" within yourself. The results will be remarkable.

experimenting with intimacy

First, go back to chapter 15 and reread the section on ki meditation (pages 148–50). Remember how you went deep within yourself, and then expanded out to fill the largest possible space? Then you came back to yourself, deep into yourself, and went out again. The capacity to move in and out like this helps you to develop discriminating awareness. You are able to move smoothly from a focus on yourself to a focus on things outside yourself. This ability is essential in all good relationships.

1. Begin your meditation.

2. As you breathe, begin the ki meditation process.

3. As you go out from yourself, take the feeling of who you really are along with you.

4. As your awareness expands, notice what people enter your awareness. They may be people you already know, or they may be people you have yet to meet.

5. As you move into yourself and out again, notice the people whom you perceive. Notice their physical appearance, their social demeanor, and the emotional tone you feel when you are close to them.

6. As you go back within yourself, take one of them with you. Notice how it feels to have this person close to you. If there are other people in your awareness, try

this with each one. Notice how each one feels different, unique.

7. Complete your meditation.

One point of this exercise is to become familiar with
your own responses. If you tried to bring someone close
whom you don't really like, you may have felt prickly or
stiff. If the person is a good friend, you may have felt warm
and relaxed. With a soul mate, you will feel safe, warm,
and full. You will see rich, vibrant colors. You will taste
and smell something familiar. Any sounds will resonate
deep within you. You will feel totally alive.

By opening yourself to the meditation experience, you
practice opening yourself to another person. As you meet
people, you can choose to open a bit to see how it feels.
You will have experienced the "right" feeling to some
degree, and you will certainly know a "wrong" feeling
when you perceive it. In this way you will make consistently better connections with the people you meet.

If you are at the level of spiritual development where
you are seeking a soul mate, then you will find you meet
people who are on similar levels. If they are not seeking the
same things, you will feel prickly, rigid, or some other feeling you have identified as not acceptable. The interesting
thing is that other people will be going through a similar
process. They may not be conscious of what they are doing,
but they are doing some kind of sorting and evaluating too.

When you open to someone who is opening to you,
there is a rush of feelings. No more of the one-sided yearn-

ing to be seen, spoken to, or touched. No more doubts, no hesitation. Oh, the two of you may be seriously surprised and pleased. It may take awhile for you to get together, but you will know you have met a soul that resonates with yours.

It is important to remember that you don't need to have a romantic or sexual relationship with your soul mate. Your mother, your child, or your sibling could be your soul mate too. I have met one or two women with whom I resonated so strongly that I was "in love." That doesn't mean I have to sleep with each one, although any soul mate may evoke physical desire within you. I knew from the day I met my husband that he would be a lifelong friend and teacher. It wasn't until later that romance entered the picture. Your practice of openness in meditation has prepared you for such eventualities. You will be able to admire such an individual without lusting after him or her. When the physical passion finally does engage, it will raise the bar to ecstatic heights!

summary

Every relationship you have benefits from greater openness. Even if you never find your soul mate, each person you meet will be more alive and interesting to you. You will be more present for them too. By cultivating openness and compassion, you will begin to see all people in a more positive light.

Next we will consider your relationship to the Divine, and how it benefits from meditation.

23

About the Divine

Metaphysically, we recognize the Universal Spirit as the Source of all life and inspiration; as Infinite Self-Knowingness. The mind of man is an extension of the Eternal Mind or Spirit.

Ernest Holmes
The Science of Mind

THROUGHOUT THIS BOOK you have discovered many potential benefits of meditation. It improves health through relaxation and stress reduction. It promotes physical strength and flexibility through various moving meditations. It helps to develop more focused attention. It provides a way to enhance your dream life and your understanding of dreams. Meditation provides an activity that you do just for yourself, with no other considerations.

As you practice meditation, you quiet your mind. You give yourself a rest from the constant chatter you carry around with you throughout the day. This chatter even pervades your dreams. We replay problem scenarios over and over in our heads, trying to find a solution. We often turn such thought patterns into obsessions. Meditation relieves stress and some of our physical pain by quieting the chatter. By quieting the mind, we accomplish three things:

1. We turn off the tapes that play, if only temporarily.

2. We allow ourselves to mentally rest.

3. We replace the chatter with focused attention.

Focused attention, then, becomes a valuable life tool. By focusing on what we do in meditation, we learn to focus on what we do in every area of life. Focused attention helps keep us on track with everything we do, and this means that we enter into each activity more fully. Thus we become more accomplished, and we deepen the quality of each experience.

Beyond these benefits, meditation allows gaps to occur between thoughts. As you practice various meditation exercises, you have probably experienced these gaps. You become aware that there has been no thought for a moment or two—nothing, an empty space. These gaps are surprising at first. While we don't usually imagine ourselves as thinking something all the time, mental processes are in fact more or less ongoing. We change the focus moment to moment, but the movement is virtually continuous. Meditation introduces gaps as a fresh experience.

Once you have this experience, you will very likely remember other situations in which there was a gap. You may have felt it as an uncomfortable moment in which you could not remember another person's name. No mental process occurs for a moment and you are at a loss to name a person whom you have known for years. While this is not a positive experience, it is an experience of a kind of gap. Perhaps you have seen a person who is so remarkable—drop-dead gorgeous, intellectually powerful, emotionally charismatic, or spiritually brilliant—that you are stopped in your tracks. You stare, you stammer, and you are somewhat breathless. You have a completely single-minded focus on that person. You experience no mental movement, as you are 100 percent focused. This is another kind of gap. Sudden onset of grief can produce such a moment as well.

Meditation produces a spiritual gap. When a moment of mental stillness occurs in meditation, you are then open for new information to arise. Some of what comes up will be ordinary information—a solution to a problem you are working on, insights into a relationship—but some of what comes to you in those moments is powerful wisdom of a spiritual nature. Where does this wisdom come from, and what is it?

- **Your own intuition and intellect may combine to resolve a question.** This is a process of your own mind. Intuition is hampered by the constant chatter you have been observing in your meditation. As you learn to still your mind, it is like freeing up memory in a massively powerful computer. The more space there is for your thoughts, the better job of synthesis can occur. By moving the chatter aside, or turning the volume very low, you can use the quiet time to develop themes of problem-solving and creativity using more of your own mind. Often we think of intellect and intuition as being separate functions. Through meditation you align them as partners on your creative path.

- **There is an inner wisdom that comes from your daimon, your own spirit.** We all have an inner voice. This inner voice does not go away, regardless of what we do to ignore it. It may be very quiet, unrecognizable amidst the daily chatter, but it never deserts you. Its purpose is to guide you on the best path toward your spiritual expression. When you meditate, you enter a stillness in which the voice can be clearly heard. The spirit within you may be heard, or seen, or felt in the body. This voice has the wisdom of the ages, even in small children. As you reach maturity, it can become your best friend, or it can be perceived as an eternal pest—or it can be very, very quiet. Meditation helps you learn how to pay attention and respond to this inner expression of your spirit.

- **In addition to your own wisdom, there is an intelligence that pervades the world.** Beyond your inner voice, you can perceive this larger mind. Some people call this the Planet Mind. We personify this mind as Mother Earth, for example. There was once a margarine commercial that stated, "Don't mess with Mother Nature." That statement could have come to the writer in meditation. It is the sort of straightforward message that people often get through meditation. Even when the message seems obvious, you find that it also has the ring of profound truth.

Some people think of this source as Universal Mind. Just as your mind keeps you constantly busy with a flow of information, Universal Mind is constantly flowing, guiding, nudging, and even pushing us in various directions. By definition, all things exist in Universal Mind. The past, present, and future are there. All hopes, sorrows, and aspirations can be said to exist in Universal Mind. Because it is there, we are capable of perceiving its workings all the time. Generally, though, we are too busy with other thoughts. Meditation opens us to the experience more directly, and trains us to develop easier access to this source of wisdom.

- **We can receive direct transmission from another mind.** You have heard of telepathy, clairvoyance, and other means of knowing that do not come through ordinary means. Direct transmission is such a means. Normally, a teacher conveys a lesson through words, images, sound, or touch. A chef even uses taste to teach his or her students. However, in addition, your teacher may also contact your mind directly, without the need of the normal senses. Through this direct contact, you absorb the meaning of the lesson without the necessity of filtering it the usual way.

Such transmissions can come from a teacher whom you have sought, or they can come from a source that is seeking you out. Channelers have written about a source in the distant Pleiades, a group of stars in the constellation of Taurus. This source is apparently sending a consistent message to a number of people who are open to hear it. Alice Bailey wrote volumes about her source the Tibetan, an ascended master.

- **Information comes direct from God or Goddess.** Prophets hear the word of God and share it with their followers. Shamans use this kind of direct contact with the larger source to effect healings. Many religious practices are designed to allow the voice of the Divine to enter into you directly. The world is rich with mythologies that explain the nature of gods and goddesses, and record their interactions with humanity. We pray—for a vision, guidance, comfort, wisdom—to a god or goddess whom we have personified to make the connection more poignant.

- **Sometimes angels appear to people in near-blinding glory.** Their appearance can only be described as life-changing. Sometimes they speak to you with a quiet voice that may only be heard in meditation. An angel uses the voice and the appearance that will work best for you.

  I recall a story a friend told me. Once when she was at a very low point in her life, so low that she didn't see how she could continue living, she went into a church to sit and pray. She said that she was even beyond prayer, her despair was so deep. As she sat there, an ordinary-looking woman appeared by her side. She did not hear this woman's steps on the bare floor of the aisle; the woman was simply there. The woman didn't say anything, but a sense of well-being pervaded the space around the two of them. My friend felt calm, quiet assurance coming from this woman. After a few moments she noticed that the woman was gone, just as silently as she had come.

Who was the woman? My friend was certain that she was the Virgin Mary. Another person would have seen her as an angel. Another would have seen her as an expression of the Goddess. Some would have seen her as an ordinary woman who just happened to be very quiet and very serene. It doesn't really matter whether she was a vision, a real entity, or an ordinary person. My friend, even in her despair, was still enough that a powerful force entered her experience that day. That force gave her the strength to continue living, to find a path out of her desperate circumstances. It also revealed my friend's profound capacity for compassion. Since that time she has earned a master's degree in psychology and gone on to help hundreds or thousands of people find their way out of despair.

While most of us may not have such an intense experience, we all can benefit from opening to more spiritual experiences. We are physically healthier when we relate to the world through positive, nourishing activities. We are mentally healthier when we train our minds to focus clearly and to think clearly. We are emotionally healthier when we communicate well with other people and resolve issues that otherwise continue to plague our thoughts. Spiritual health is really no different. As we open to the possibility of the Divine, we are enriched in ways that money cannot touch.

perceiving the divine

1. Enter your meditation as usual.

2. Breathe deeply and rhythmically, and relax into a comfortable meditation.

3. Continue for a comfortable period of time.

4. Notice what thoughts or feelings arise during the meditation.

What did you experience? A slight cramp in your calf? A bright color in your field of vision? A face or a figure? Thoughts about the work you need to accomplish today? Whatever you experienced, it is both a part of you and an expression of the Divine. It is a part of you because you have experienced it, if for no other reason. It is an expression of the Divine because everything you experience is part of that expression. Don't discount your experience as meaningless. All life has meaning and value, though we may not be able to understand it.

I often find my mind wandering as I try to meditate. I am sometimes surprised at the variety of thoughts that can arise to keep me busy. I also find that eventually I have a thought about another person, or a group of people who are struggling with a problem. When that happens, I find that I literally warm up to compassionate thoughts about them. I perceive the difficulty, and I wish for the ability to help. Now I know I cannot always help directly. However, I believe that by holding such a person or group in compassionate thought, they are spiritually uplifted. Prayers work, treatments work, mantras work, and spells work. All of these help us to connect with the Divine in positive, creative ways. The exact words are not as important as the intention, although certain words do appear to have very strong impact. For me it is the compassionate thought that provides the most direct, most powerful connection.

_____summary

It is my personal belief that each of us is unique, and therefore has a unique connection to the Divine. We do not need one single, rigid, defining religious path. What we need is a personal, flexible, open, spiritual persona. Many of us find spiritual support in churches or circles or sets of beliefs. That is a testament to what we share as human beings. In the differences of thought and feeling, each of you pursues a unique path toward spirit. Meditation can be both guide and servant along that path.

Space and Clarity

There is a looker-on who sits behind my eyes. It seems he has seen things in ages and world beyond memory's shore, and those forgotten sights glisten on the grass and shiver on the leaves. He has seen under new veils the face of the one beloved, in twilight hours of many a nameless star. Therefore his sky seems to ache with the pain of countless meetings and partings, and a longing pervades this spring breeze—the longing that is full of the whisper of ages without beginning.

Rabindranath Tagore
The Collected Poems and Plays

YOU BEGAN READING this book with some idea of what you hoped to gain from meditation. You have, hopefully, tried a number of the exercises and found several that resonate with you. You have established a meditation practice, finding a few minutes each day (or nearly every day) to spend with yourself, for yourself. You are gaining an understanding of meditation, and you are learning about yourself.

231

Space and Clarity

You need space to become clear.

Think of a fishing net, all folded up into a bundle. It is hard even to see what it is. Imagine that you are looking for a hole in the net so that you can mend it. You must spread the net out and examine it carefully. You find the hole in the net and repair it. While you are at it, you find any weak places in the net. You repair them before they break. Now you are ready for the next big catch.

Your meditation process is much the same as this. You create the space in which to examine your physical, mental, emotional, and spiritual being. You examine your mind. You make friends with yourself, and you make changes in the way you view yourself. Then you can change the world in ways you never believed possible.

Glossary

ADHD (Attention Deficit Hyperactivity Disorder)—A brain disorder that results in a state of distraction by unimportant sights and sounds, in which the mind drives you from one thought or activity to the next. It also immerses you so deeply in thoughts and images that you don't notice when someone speaks to you.

Archetype—A pre-existent form, such as a mythological theme, a visual shape, or concept, which spontaneously arises in dreams or waking life without having been experienced before in one's consciousness. Archetypal forms and patterns may be transmitted by tradition or migration of social groups. They are fundamentally transmitted via heredity and may be experienced apart from education, tradition, or other conscious means.

Asana—A posture in yoga.

Chakra—Sanskrit word for "wheel" or "disk." The term usually refers to one of seven basic energy centers in the body, which correspond to nerve centers or ganglia. In addition, the chakras also reflect levels of consciousness.

Daimon—The voice within each of us; our unique personal source of inspiration and enlightenment.

Eightfold Path—The Buddhist way to self-realization. The eight behaviors are as follows: (1) right understanding; (2) right intention, or thought; (3) right action; (4) right speech; (5) right livelihood; (6) right effort; (7) right mindfulness; and (8) right concentration.

Four Noble Truths—Basic precepts of Buddhism. They include: (1) there is suffering in the world; (2) there is a cause of suffering; (3) there is an end to suffering, and (4) we can follow the path to end suffering by destroying ignorance.

Gomden—A very firm, rectangular cushion about six inches thick.

Kriya—A set of yogic and/or meditative exercises.

Kundalini—Kundalini is a word used to describe the creative energy each person possesses. This creative energy is largely dormant until it is aroused, either incidentally or through intentional meditation and yoga practice.

Kundalini yoga is a systematic practice that stimulates the glandular system and strengthens the body. The practice includes breath work, chanting, physical movement, yoga postures, and meditation. Many of the kriyas, or exercises, are designed to move energy through glandular or spinal centers. Through the practice you gain clarity of mind, spiritual awareness, and the capacity to understand actions and their outcomes. The result is a joining of individual awareness with universal consciousness.

Mantra—A set of specific words in a particular configuration, to be repeated in a rhythmic manner.

Mudra—A hand gesture that carries specific symbolic meaning.

Pranayama—A system of techniques for breathing and concentration, thought to confer upon its practitioner a calm, balanced, and focused mind, increased vitality, and longevity.

Shadow—A psychological term introduced by Carl G. Jung. It is everything in us that is unconscious, repressed, undeveloped, and denied. This includes both the dark, unacceptable side of our personalities and the unknown light qualities of which we are unaware.

Shamata—Calm-abiding, stabilizing meditation that involves following the breath.

Symbol—A picture, shape, or design that has a meaning that is agreed upon by one's culture in general, and sometimes across cultures.

Tantra—A method of performing worship in a systemized way.

Vippasyana—Analytical, insightful meditation, which inspires certainty and confidence and allows for intuitive insight.

Yantra—A geometric figure, usually inscribed on a metallic plate or paper, used as an object of meditation.

Zabuton—A flat cushion upon which to sit (often used under a gomden or zafu).

Zafu—A firm, round cushion about four inches thick (sometimes moon-shaped).

Bibliography

Acredolo, Linda. "Q & A with Dr. Dean Ornish," http://my.webmd.com/content/article/3079.682

Anonymous. "Karma Yoga: Path of Selfless Action." http://www.talamasca.org/avatar/yoga3.html

Bailey, Alice. *Esoteric Astrology.* New York: Lucis Publishing Company, 1979.

Bandler, Richard, and John Grinder. *Frogs into Princes: Neuro Linguistic Programming.* Moab, Utah: Real People Press, 1979.

Barbor, Cary. "The Science of Meditation," *Psychology Today* 34 (2001): 54.

Bennet, E. A. *What Jung Really Said.* New York: Schocken Books, 1967.

Bercholz, Samuel, and Sherab Chödzin Kohn, eds. *An Introduction to the Buddha and His Teachings.* New York: Barnes & Noble, 1993.

Braly, James. *Dr. Braly's Food Allergy and Nutrition Revolution: For Permanent Weight Loss and a Longer, Healthier Life.* New York: McGraw-Hill, 1992.

Clagett, Alice B., and Elandra Kirsten Meredith, comps. *Yoga for Health and Healing.* Santa Monica, Calif.: Alice Clagett, 1994.

Bibliography

Clement, Stephanie Jean, and Terry Lee Rosen. *Dreams: Working Interactive*. St. Paul, Minn.: Llewellyn, 2000.

Dalai Lama, H.H. *The Path to Tranquility*. New York: Viking, 1998.

De Bono, Edward. *Serious Creativity: Using the Power of Lateral Thinking to Create New Ideas*. New York: Harper Collins, 1992.

Frost, Robert. "Mending Wall." In *Concise Anthology of American Literature*, edited by George McMichael. 2d ed. New York: Macmillan, 1985.

Hanh, Thich Nhat. *The Heart of the Buddha's Teaching*. New York: Broadway Books, 1999.

Harrington, Jacine. *The Beauty of Yoga*. St. Paul, Minn.: Llewellyn, 2001.

Heraclitus. *Fragments*. Toronto, Canada: University of Toronto Press, 1987.

Holmes, Ernest. *The Science of Mind*. New York: Dodd, Mead and Company, 1938.

The I Ching, or Book of Changes. Translated by Richard Wilhelm. Bollingen Series, no. 19. Princeton, N.J.: Princeton University Press, 1984.

Judy, Dwight H. *Christian Meditation and Inner Healing*. New York: Crossroad, 1991.

Jung, C. G. *Mandala Symbolism*. Princeton, N.J.: Princeton University Press, 1969.

Karthar Rinpoche, Khenpo. *Dharma Paths*. Ithaca, N.Y.: Snow Lion, 1992.

———. *Transforming Mental Afflictions and Other Selected Teachings*. Big Rapids, Mich.: KTD Dharma Goods, 1997.

Bibliography

Kübler-Ross, Elisabeth. *The Wheel of Life*. New York: Touchstone, 1997.

Kumar, Ravindra. *Kundalini for Beginners*. St. Paul, Minn.: Llewellyn, 2000.

Markova, Dawna. *The Open Mind*. Berkeley, Calif.: Conari Press, 1996.

Ortega y Gasset, Jose. *Mission of the University*. New York: W. W. Norton, 1944.

Pond, David. *Chakras for Beginners*. St. Paul, Minn.: Llewellyn, 1999.

Renée, Janina. *Tarot for a New Generation*. St. Paul, Minn.: Llewellyn, 2001.

Rilke, Rainer Maria. *Sonnets to Orpheus*. New York: W. W. Norton, 1970.

———. *Translations*. Translated by M. D. Herter Norton. New York: W. W. Norton, 1993.

Rivera, Rudy. *Your Hidden Food Allergies Are Making You Fat*. New York: Prima Communications, 1998.

Singh Khalsa, M.S.S. Gurucharan. *Kundalini Yoga/Sadhana Guidelines*. Pomona, Calif.: Kundalini Research Institute, 1978.

Stuber, William. *Gems of the 7 Color Rays*. St. Paul, Minn.: Llewellyn, 2001.

Tagore, Rabindranath. *The Collected Poems and Plays*. New York: Macmillan, 1993.

Tohei, Koichi. *Ki in Daily Life*. Tokyo: Japan Publications, 2001.

Trungpa Rinpoche, Chogyam. *Meditation in Action*. Berkeley, Calif.: Shambhala, 1969.

Bibliography

Vennells, David, F. *Reflexology for Beginners*. St. Paul, Minn.: Llewellyn, 2001.

———. *Reiki for Beginners*. St. Paul, Minn.: Llewellyn, 1999.

Wenger, Silvia. "The Training of Attention and Unconditional Presence in Dance/Movement Therapy." Master's thesis, Naropa Institute, 1989.

Wilber, Ken. *Eye to Eye*. New York: Doubleday, 1983.

———. *Up from Eden*. New York: Doubleday, 1981.

Index

Index

GET MORE AT LLEWELLYN.COM

Visit us online to browse hundreds of our books and decks, plus sign up to receive our e-newsletters and exclusive online offers.

- **Free tarot readings • Spell-a-Day • Moon phases**
- **Recipes, spells, and tips • Blogs • Encyclopedia**
- **Author interviews, articles, and upcoming events**

GET SOCIAL WITH LLEWELLYN

Find us on
Facebook
www.Facebook.com/LlewellynBooks

Follow us on
twitter™
www.Twitter.com/Llewellynbooks

GET BOOKS AT LLEWELLYN

LLEWELLYN ORDERING INFORMATION

Order online: Visit our website at www.llewellyn.com to select your books and place an order on our secure server.

Order by phone:
- Call toll-free within the U.S. at 1-877-NEW-WRLD (1-877-639-9753)
- Call toll free within Canada at 1-866-NEW-WRLD (1-866-639-9753)
- We accept VISA, MasterCard, and American Express

Order by mail:
Send the full price of your order (MN residents add 6.875% sales tax) in U.S. funds, plus postage and handling to: Llewellyn Worldwide, 2143 Wooddale Drive Woodbury, MN 55125-2989

POSTAGE AND HANDLING:

STANDARD: (U.S., Mexico & Canada)
(Please allow 2 business days)
$25.00 and under, add $4.00.
$25.01 and over, FREE SHIPPING.

INTERNATIONAL ORDERS (airmail only):
$16.00 for one book, plus $3.00 for each additional book.

Visit us online for more shipping options. Prices subject to change.

FREE CATALOG!

To order, call
1-877-
NEW-WRLD
ext. 8236
or visit our
website

Meditation as Spiritual Practice
GENEVIEVE L. PAULSON , PH.D

Meditation has many purposes: healing, past life awareness, mental clarity, and relaxation. This practice can also enhance our spiritual lives by bringing about "peak experiences" or transcendental states. *Meditation as Spiritual Practice* focuses on the practice of meditation for expanding consciousness and awareness. The techniques in this treasured guidebook can also help one in developing clairvoyance, clairaudience, and other psychic abilities.

Discover for yourself how the power of meditation can expand your mind, heal your body, and lift your spirit.

0-7387-0851-8
Illus., bibliog., index $14.95

To order, call 1-877-NEW-WRLD
Prices subject to change without notice

Compose Yourself!
Awakening to the Rhythms of Life

ANDY BARNETT

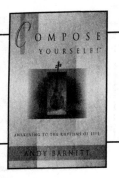

Even if you can't sing or play an instrument, you can use the musical model presented in *Compose Yourself!* to create a more harmonious life. Whether you know a little or a lot about the structure of musical compositions, these same principles can be applied to every aspect of your life. Using musical intent can transform your personal interactions into sweet duets and your work into a melodic theme of self-expression.

Learn how to bring musical intent to everything you do. Fun, simple exercises throughout the book will help you joyfully bring harmony to all aspects of your life. Using your innate musicality to work with the ancient Vedic system of the chakras, you can strengthen your body, deepen your breath, open your heart, fine-tune your hearing, and sharpen your wit.

0-7387-0418-0 $16.95

Authentic Spirituality
The Direct Path to Consciousness
RICHARD POTTER

The idea that any one religion has a monopoly on the divine is a concept that has led to bigotry, bloodshed, and war throughout both the ancient and modern world.

The time has come for a spirituality of consciousness. By focusing on consciousness instead of dogma, it becomes possible to realize the core truths of world religions without being bound to outdated beliefs and customs that no longer serve humanity.

Learn core consciousness-expanding practices including meditation, breathwork, sound work, and retreats. Explore ways to open your heart, achieve self mastery, evaluate spiritual teachers, and attain spiritual freedom, all steps on the path to greater contentment, clarity, compassion, and a profound sense of inner peace.

Take a spiritual adventure beyond the bounds of time and place with one of today's most original spiritual thinkers.

0-7387-0442-3 $15.95